Full Circle
Spiritual Therapy for the Elderly

HAWORTH Activities Management
Phyllis M. Foster
Senior Editor

A Practical Guide to Art Therapy Groups by Diane Fausek

Television in the Nursing Home: A Case Study of Media Consumption Routines and Strategies of Nursing Home Residents by Wendy J. Hajjar

Full Circle: Spiritual Therapy for the Elderly by Kevin Kirkland and Howard McIlveen

Additional Titles of Related Interest:

Occupational and Physical Therapy in Educational Environments edited by Irene R. McEwen

Creative Arts with Older People edited by Janice McMurray

Activities and the "Well Elderly" edited by Phyllis Foster

Activities with Developmentally Disabled Elderly and Older Adults edited by M. Jean Keller

Educational Activity Programs for Older Adults: A 12-Month Idea Guide for Adult Education Instructors and Activity Directors in Gerontology by Janice Lake Williams and Janet Downs

Handbook of Group Activities for Impaired Adults by Elsbeth Martindale and Scott Cabot Willis

You Bring Out the Music in Me: Music in Nursing Homes edited by Beckie Karras

From Deep Within: Poetry Workshops in Nursing Homes edited by Carol F. Peck

Full Circle
Spiritual Therapy for the Elderly

Kevin Kirkland, BMus, MTA
Howard McIlveen, BA, MDiv

Routledge
Taylor & Francis Group
New York London

The Haworth Press, Inc., 10 Alice Street, Binghamton, NY 13904-1580

Softcover edition published 2000.

Cover design by Jennifer M. Gaska.

The Library of Congress has cataloged the hardcover edition of this book as:

Kirkland, Kevin H., 1963-
    Full circle : spiritual therapy for the elderly / Kevin Kirkland, Howard McIlveen.
        p.   cm.
    Includes bibliographical references and index.
    ISBN 0-7890-0606-5 (alk. paper)
    1. Church work with nursing home patients. 2. Senile dementia—Patients—Religious life. 3. Music therapy for the aged. 4. Worship programs. I. McIlveen, Howard. II. Title.
BV4435.5.K57 1999
259'.3—dc21   98-28109
                                                                                              CIP

ISBN 0-7890-0607-3 (pbk.)

CONTENTS

ABOUT THE AUTHORS

Kevin Kirkland is an accredited music therapist working with the elderly at the University of British Columbia Hospital and at Yaletown House in Vancouver. He trained in music therapy at Capilano College and completed an MA from California State University. He is past president of both the Music Therapy Association of British Columbia and the Canadian Association for Music Therapy.

Howard McIlveen, a CAPPE certified chaplain specializing in hospital ministry, is the Pastoral Care Coordinator of Vancouver's Richmond Hospital. Mr. McIlveen has been involved with the cognitively impaired elderly since 1991, working in an inner-city mission and as a congregational minister.

Preface

Howard: The program that this manual seeks to describe evolved in a long-term care facility in Richmond, BC, Canada. Kevin had been there for three years, working largely with special care residents, i.e., residents with dementia. I was new to the facility and, frankly, was groping to find a way of being chaplain to the cognitively impaired. About a month after I had started at this nursing home, it was part of an accreditation survey. In Canada, that consists of an assessment of the institution which can happen at two-, three-, or four-year intervals, depending on the rating they give you. The survey is overseen by a national accrediting body and is carried out on location by a surveyor from another part of the country. When the surveyor heard separately from Kevin and me about our aspirations and ideas, she wholeheartedly supported and challenged us both to "get on with it."

So in the summer of 1991, we began with a weekly group. We found as we went along that we enjoyed each other and the group of residents; in fact, even with some memorable fiascoes, this group was the highlight of our week. More important, after a few months of "settling," we were seeing change in the residents.

In September 1993, I became the chaplain of the Richmond Hospital. By this time, we had talked and written about our program. We were impressed with the enthusiasm of the response both from professionals and laypeople alike. When I arrived at the Richmond Hospital, the music therapist, who had heard of *Full Circle* ™, was eager to begin immediately with me as co-therapist. We noticed significant changes in the behavior of the special care residents who came to our group. There was less weepiness on the ward, fewer outbursts, decreased wandering, a presenting sense of belonging and friendship with the other residents, and a cessation of talking about past problems or a decrease in emotional response to them. As we witnessed the effects of *Full Circle* on our residents, the importance of their feeling the support and presence of God and their belief system became more and more apparent. The comfort this brings is a basic need.

Since that time I have co-led the program in three intermediate care residences. I have now completed three years of developing this program in an extended care residence in cooperation with two music therapists, Julia South Lattimer and Eudora Ng. Kevin and I have conducted training in the program for co-professionals. It was featured in the Canadian national chaplaincy newsletter. At every point, we have received affirmation that this is an approach which is needed and that there are others who are willing to run with it.

Among the dementias in our society, that of the Alzheimer type is the most prominent. Along with the growing awareness of its existence, there seems to be a growing incidence of the disease. It is hard to imagine a disease that is more dispiriting to families and cruel to the patient. We find that among professional medical people who care for these patients, the focus is on the lacks and the losses. Although what is reflected in this book is not a panacea, we are able and eager to say, on the basis of seven years experience, that we do see positive changes in people with dementia. More specifically, we see growth.

We are hopeful that others, through this book, will catch the vision of what can be. We write particularly with pastoral care and music therapy providers in mind; however, administrators, recreation programmers, and even family members of the cognitively impaired will find direction and hope through this book.

Kevin: This is a how-to book for enriching the spiritual lives of the elderly and those caring for them. We've called it "spiritual therapy" because it is a program for facilitating healing, resolution, remembering, and experiencing of the sacred, the complete, the joyous, the whole. Spiritual therapy is many things. It is the experience of sitting in a circle together, holding hands in song. It is an effable feeling that arises from celebrating the human spirit together, where music uplifts, where faith provides comfort. It is as simple as a childhood memory, a smile, or the soft singing of a familiar hymn. It is about kinship, reminiscing, and coming to know about the biographies of those in the group. You could say it is about soul.

For many seniors, religion has always been an important element of their lives. Yet, here we were, Howard and I, working in a long-term care facility and realizing that for many of these people, especially those on a locked special care or so-called dementia unit, there was little opportunity to express their religious spirit, to attend a church service, or to be treated as a whole person, as someone who can still think, feel, learn, and grow.

A rapidly growing body of evidence is unfolding concerning the importance of addressing and facilitating the spiritual needs of the elderly. Koenig writes, ". . . religious attitudes, beliefs, and coping behaviors are, in general, positively related to mental health in older adults," and "Amount of pain experienced was significantly lower among patients scoring high in religious beliefs and among frequent church attenders, compared with others."[1] Young concurs, noting "Church attendance, prayer, and religion have been found to enhance the quality of life for older adults, leading to a more positive attitude toward aging, as well as increasing feelings of self-worth and life satisfaction."[2] Four areas of client need have been recognized: relatedness, caring, memory (identity), and grief. Relatedness refers to a feeling of connection to a higher force through love of people who reach out to them. Caring comes through listening, validating, and nonverbal communication. Memory, as discussed in the introduction, refers to the spiritual memories people have that are unlocked through music, images, and symbols. Grief over past losses may surface. Caregivers are reminded that "memories of the death of a spouse, child, or parent may be as fresh as they were years earlier."[3]

Carr believes that every human being has a spiritual dimension and says, "To reach the stage of self-actualization or personal integrity, the older person must confront issues of meaning, loss, forgiveness, and ultimately death. These great human issues or questions challenge the elderly to explore the spiritual dimensions of life."[4] Peter Yuchi Clark identifies six areas of need for the mentally ill elderly in *The Journal of Pastoral Care:*

1. *Somatic.* "For an aging, mentally ill person who is concerned about what may be going 'wrong' with the body or mind, the elements of worship which relate to body function may have more meaning."[5] We have included somatic themes to address these areas: Legs and Feet, Arms, Sight (Eyes), Hearing (Ears), Hands/Touch, Voice (Mouth), and Faces.

2. *Illness as a curse and the need for blessing.* ". . . people have a strong need for acceptance, and yet in their brokenness they feel rejection. Stigmas of being mentally ill, of being old, and problem of not being in control." A worship service "can provide opportunities for people to receive a blessing which can aid them in coping with a (seemingly) curse-laden life situation."[6] Themes we have explored include Healing, Forgiveness, Transition/Moves, Memories and Memories Lost, Prayer, and Trust.

3. *Despair.* Worship offers the recovery and nurturing of hope. "One way in which hope can be restored is through the process of life review. Recalling life events can help aging people to discover their meaning and purpose, and give opportunities for repentance."[7] Themes dealing with this topic include Hope, Encouragement, Darkness, Change, Light, Renewal, and Freedom.

4. *Dread.* Dread is "an honest confrontation with the forces of good and evil that swirl around us."[8] The fear of death and the realities of life can be explored through themes such as Death, the Cross, Funeral Arrangements, Fear, Rest, Peace, Resurrection/New Life, and Time of one's death.

5. *Personal isolation and loneliness.* People yearn to feel a sense of belonging. Group worship enhances awareness of universality through the sharing of feelings and thoughts and fosters cohesiveness. "If one fears that one does not have enough faith, a common worship experience can provide consolation that there is enough faith within the community for all."[9] Related themes include Love, Friendship, Support, Togetherness/Unity, Children, God, and Communion.

6. *Balancing the need for personal spirituality with structure in daily life.* Expressing personal spirituality openly promotes a

sense of living in a reliable, trustworthy world and establishes a sense of structure in their daily lives.[10]

Expression of spirituality and faith is not only good for emotional well-being, it is good for the body as well. Recent research reported in the *International Journal of Psychiatry in Medicine* found ". . . that people who attend weekly services have healthier immune systems than those who don't." Interleukin 6 (IL-6) blood levels are typically higher in those with Alzheimer's, depression, AIDS, and other illnesses. And ". . . those who attended a weekly service were half as likely as nonattenders to have elevated IL-6 levels."[11] It reminds one of the old adage, "What's good for the body is good for the soul."

Music is often described as the art that arouses deep religious feelings. By "religious," of course, I mean a sense of the sacred, of the spiritual, of the atonement—whatever terminology with which the audience is most comfortable. We're so politically correct these days that the word "religion" has almost gone out of favor, even though it is a major aspect of this book. Our spiritual therapy approach is many things, really: pastoral care, music therapy, personal growth, faith, religion, activity, ministry, socialization, human compassion, palliative care, love. In writing this book, we tried to provide an extensive assortment of hymns, according to each theme, that stem from a variety of faiths and backgrounds. We also listed secular songs for those who might connect better with a song of that nature or because the lyrics simply expressed the theme best. Music therapy is well documented as one of the most successful interventions with the elderly. In our groups, we used the same song ("This Is the Day") to open each session and also used a different song to close each session. The lyrics to songs are more readily remembered than spoken language, and the feelings aroused from the associations and memories to the music are a vital element of the group experience.

The potential of those with dementia is profound. Given the opportunity for normalization, they can become insightful and coherent. They can change, and they can learn. Many do not remember what we've been talking about five minutes after the conversation, but many did know what we were talking about at that particular moment and can experience the feeling, resolution, or change in that moment.

In the introduction, we describe how we operated this program. The book itself includes over seventy-five theme-developed plans, including sacred and secular music, stories, quotations, questions for response and discussion, and prayers. About ten of the themes have been supplemented with material that could be easily adapted to a "higher-achieving" group of people. The book concludes with a bibliography that provides sources for our quotations, prayers, and music.

We hope that you take advantage of the many themes in this book to enhance the care you provide to both individuals and groups. Be as creative as you like in adapting them for your own use. May reading this book prove informative, enlightening, and encouraging to you. We hope the experiences that arise from your use of this book are as rich and rewarding as they have been, and continue to be, for us.

Howard McIlveen
Kevin Kirkland

NOTES

1. Koenig, Harold G. (1990). "Research on religion and mental health in later life: A review and commentary," *Journal of Geriatric Psychiatry,* 23(1), pp. 33 and 38.

2. Young, Cathy (1993). "Spirituality and the chronically ill Christian elderly," *Geriatric Nursing,* November/December, pp. 298-299.

3. Heriot, Cathy S. (1992). "Spirituality and aging," *Holistic Nursing Practice,* 7(1), p. 29.

4. Carr, Katherine K. (1993). "Integration of spirituality of aging into a nursing curriculum," *Gerontology and Geriatrics Education,* 13(3), p. 37.

5. Clark, Peter Yuichi (1993). "A liturgical journey at Wesley Woods: Worship experiences within an inpatient geriatric psychiatric unit," *The Journal of Pastoral Care,* 47(4), p. 392.

6. Ibid., p. 393.

7. Ibid.

8. Ibid.

9. Ibid.

10. Ibid., p. 394.

11. Atkinson, Steve (1998). "Churchgoers live longer, are happier," *Nanaimo Daily News,* July 4, p. D7.

Introduction

This book is based on a series of sessions that originated in the facility where the authors worked and also through subsequent work at other facilities. It developed out of the need for a therapy group, in which the residents are able to come *full circle* to the faith that was and is important to them—a remembrance of life experiences, their relationship to others and to God, and the familiar feelings of comfort and love that lie waiting to be awakened through their spirituality. This is how the idea of *Full Circle* came into being.

DEFINITIONS

Music therapy is one of the most successful interventions used in long-term care settings. It is generally defined as "the skillful use of music as a therapeutic tool to restore, maintain, and improve mental, physical, emotional, and spiritual health. The nonverbal, creative, and affective nature of music facilitates contact, self-expression, communication, and growth."[1]

The role of the chaplain ("chaplain," as used here, recognizes also the roles of priest, minister, or other clerical positions) in long-term care settings is ever increasing. The chaplain often contributes much more now than the traditional Sunday services and religious holiday sermons. For the elderly, perhaps more so than any other age group, religion, faith, or spirituality—whatever term one prefers—is a very important element of their lives. M. Philibert, quoted in an article titled "Spirituality and Aging," states, "aging is a spiritual rather than a biological process."[2] Koenig also notes the importance of religion in the lives of the elderly: "The research suggests that religious beliefs and behaviors of older adults based in the Judeo-Christian tradition may be associated with higher life satisfaction, sense of well-being, fewer depressive symptoms, less disability and perception of pain, and better adjustment."[3] Who is better qualified to meet the many needs of the elderly and their supportive staff than a chaplain?

Robin Nikles' article "Integration of Music Therapy and Theology: A Preliminary Approach" discusses *psychotheology*, defining it as "that discipline which seeks to integrate the fields of psychology and theology. Its ultimate purpose is to enable each field to more effectively facilitate those changes which bring individuals into a state of spiritual and psychological wholeness."[4]

RATIONALE

For many elderly, religion has always been an important aspect of their lives, and in their later years, it can provide a vehicle for recalling the past and creating feelings of spiritual fulfillment, comfort, and familiarity. These people sometimes have difficulty expressing themselves; often they feel confused and anxious. Sadly, they are sometimes treated like children. Problems and sorrows they experienced during earlier years may still need resolution and healing; they need to resolve life and prepare for death. Yet often, they are unable or lack the opportunity to participate in regular church services; a few may have even forgotten who Jesus is. But the biblical stories and hymns can evoke forgotten memories—at a feeling or spiritual level, if not a cognitive level. Some of our group participants felt as if they were attending church and were clearly pleased. Although we had no chapel, no stained glass windows, and no altar, in our own unique way, we had created a church. Cathy Heriot, in *Holistic Nursing Practice,* supports this, stating, "clients with dementia may have spiritual memories that go back to a much earlier time. . . . Music, pictures, and religious symbols may be the keys to accessing the person's memory."[5]

Our experience in working with this population is that problems and sorrows unresolved from early in life will present themselves once dementia has set in. All those social rules we learn—not to express negative feelings, not to discuss painful events, not to express doubts or fears—these barriers come down with dementia. You simply cannot consciously or unconsciously repress those feelings and thoughts. Persons with advanced dementia need the comfort that religious life has always provided them to resolve life and prepare for death. Treat them with respect, love, kindness, and patience—treat them as whole persons.

Most interventions to aid older adults to nurture their spirits involve them in reflecting on their lives. Reflective interventions usually entail eliciting older adults' life stories through a variety of methods. Reflective techniques include life review, guided autobiographies, and eliciting stories in an unstructured way. Stimulation of life memories provides older adults with an opportunity to work through their losses and maintain self-esteem, to come to grips with guilt and regrets, and to emerge feeling good about themselves.[6]

Full Circle provides many opportunities for life review through the exploration of themes such as birth, children, transitions, mother, and home. Many of the others can be used as stepping stones for recalling the past and sparking memories.

FORMAT OF THE SESSIONS

We met each Wednesday morning in the comfort of a lounge that was designated for our weekly get-togethers. Howard and I assisted six to eight special care unit residents in joining us for an hour of music, touch, story, discussion, prayer, and togetherness. The chairs were set up in a circle, with spaces left for those in wheelchairs. We put together themes which seemed important for the group to discuss or which related to a particular issue of the group or a certain individual. This group soon became the highlight of the week. Some folks think that people with Alzheimer's are incapable of insight, growth, and change. Think again. Some of their responses are profoundly lucid and rational, some are metaphoric or symbolic, and of course, some appear to make no sense at all—but all group members are respected and appreciated for their level of involvement and input. The clients' names used in our examples have been changed, and personalized accounts have been altered to protect anonymity.

Opening Song

We always start with the same welcoming song, "This Is the Day," and sometimes even before we've sung it, Nan will say "This is the day," just as I'm settling into a chair with my guitar, her memory triggered by the continuity of our get-togethers. For the second verse, we made up our own words, singing "These are my friends that the Lord has given," both of us making eye contact with the group, while Howard reaches out to shake hands with the group members. Then we do a round to greet each person individually. We ask all members how they're doing and have them introduce themselves to their neighbor and shake hands—a means of increasing group awareness. Sometimes we chat generally, and the theme of the day naturally evolves from the conversation. When this doesn't happen, we either subtly introduce it or announce, "Today let's talk about . . .".

Music

Selections of hymns and/or secular songs are interspersed with dialogue. The words to the songs are always useful for keeping the theme alive and for contemplating what the songs mean. Also, for those with dementia, music (familiar and unfamiliar) holds the attention of the group. We generally avoid handing out song sheets with large-print words, as this tends to be distracting and is usually difficult for them to follow. Occasionally, the facilitators will share their copy of the music with the person beside them.

Theme for Each Week

The themes for each week tie in to every aspect: the hymns and song, the stories and discussion, the quotations, the poetry, the prayers. The stories can be a focal point to the discussion or simply a means of enhancing some reminiscence before moving on. Both biblical and secular stories are used, and of course you might have stories of your own you know of that could well be used too. A great Web site that has short daily stories and messages is called "Our Daily Bread," produced by RBC Ministries.

Sometimes the theme we've gone to such trouble to prepare is completely off for that day and must be set aside. Always be willing to disregard your agenda in favor of a topic that is more suitable to the present situation. Having your book of hymns handy and being familiar with them will help you work with the group on the spur of the moment. Questions to be explored with the group are prepared according to the theme. Sensory cues are also used to add further stimulation. For example, in presenting the theme of "Light," we placed a candle in the middle of the circle; this really focused their attention. We began the group on "Celebration" by tossing a balloon back and forth to lively music.

Another time, we used the theme "Change," incorporating the hymns "Abide with Me," "His Eye Is on the Sparrow," "Just as I Am," "The Servant Song," and "Rock of Ages." Questions we had prepared included, "What important changes occurred in your life?" We related this to physical, emotional, and environmental changes. We also asked, "Who has helped you make changes in your life?" and "How do you deal with change?" If you've known the group for a while, you can compliment each individual on a positive change you've seen in her or him.

In keeping with the Change theme, the chaplain collected some old pictures of the residents from their families. For Phyllis, often quiet and withdrawn in the group, one picture reminded her of being in Bermuda with her husband and of his death from amyotrophic lateral sclerosis (ALS), commonly called Lou Gehrig's disease. She also remembered her mother being a very fussy and cold, domineering woman. It was a relief for Phyllis to move to Canada and get away from her demanding mother. Her feelings were validated through group support and tied into the hymn "Abide with Me."

Nan related that moving to Canada was the biggest change for her; she had to make a life of her own, and she found it difficult to leave her four brothers and her mother. Vera, who has had difficulty processing her daughter's death a couple of years ago, talked about Annalee's illness as a big change in her life. Still, Vera felt that we remain basically the same person throughout change. Her memory of Annalee was paired with the hymn "His Eye Is on the Sparrow," which everyone sang. Betty was tired and somewhat confused, but she did sing along with the hymns. We talked about accepting one another as we are and that they are loved just as they are—an important message for those with dementia, who may on some level be feeling inadequate, incomplete, or unloved. On more than one occasion, I've emphasized this point with a resident: "I love you just the way you are," or "I love you for who you are," or "You are loved for being you." "Just as I Am" was of course the song used here, though it would have been possible to have used Billy Joel's song "Just the Way You Are" or other songs with related lyrics. We find it's most beneficial to play songs that are likely to be familiar and personally meaningful to the residents. For the prayer, Howard touched upon the changes each resident has made in her or his life, ending with this familiar prayer:

> God, give us grace to accept with serenity the things that cannot be changed, courage to change the things that should be changed, and the wisdom to distinguish the one from the other.

> *Reinhold Niebuhr*

Prayer

Prayer may be described as "humanity's conscious relationship with God . . . the concept of prayer is traditionally divided into praise, thanksgiving, confession, and supplication . . ."[7] After discussions and hymns we pause for a prayer, asking, and sometimes assisting, each member to join hands in a full circle. If someone isn't in the mood to hold hands, that's fine too. Most often everyone participates, and the chaplain leads them in a prayer that relates to the topic of the day and to what individuals have said or need. Sometimes we recite the Lord's Prayer—forever memorable.

Closing and Refreshment

After the prayer, we often continue to hold hands and sing, without music (a cappella), the closing song, "God Be with You Till We Meet Again." The sense of community and togetherness is apparent. We would then thank them for having attended group and assist them in returning to the ward for juice or a hot cup of tea or coffee.

Note Taking

One of our most important investments is the time that we the staff members spend together after the group disperses. We meet, if possible, immediately following the group experience. For twenty to forty minutes, we assess the group dynamics and each person's awareness of other individuals and any gestures of socialization. During sessions, we track the response of the very restless or the perseverators, and we note interventions on our part that did or did not work. What we have written in previous sessions can be used as a basis for comparison with today's experience.

We may make note of a specific verbal response that an individual has made or whether the resident has sung, with or without cuing. We watch faces closely for signs of discomfort (sometimes alleviated by repositioning the person in her or his chair) but also for flickers or floods of emotional response.

Occasionally, words emerge where they have not been present before or where they have been scarce. Sometimes those words open up a present or past distress to which we can respond by holding or praying for the person. On one occasion, on November 11, I asked group members if any of them had experienced the death of someone close to them during wartime. A man, whose speech rarely made sense to us, shared memories about his brother's death in France—one week before the end of World War I; he wept as he told us the details. We ministered to him through music, touch, and prayer, but we also noted the details in our ever-ready notebooks.

These notes are a treasure of abilities, skills, and communication—treasures that we share intermittently with other staff and families. They sometimes supply much-needed encouragement at case conferences.

Session Examples: Parents and Home

The two themes "Parents" and "Home" brought a flood of memories from our group. Songs such as "Bless This House," "He," "Softly and Tenderly Jesus Is Calling," "Jesus Loves Me" and "Ave Maria" were the stepping stones for discussion. For example, "What do you remember about your home?" and "Betty, tell us about your mother." Because those with dementia often believe their parents are still alive, "Tell us about your mother" avoids using the past tense, leaving it open for any response. In our group, everyone reminisced about their homes, the love of mothers, fathers, and family life. Nan recalled her four brothers and their "humble home" full of love. When asked if anyone owned a gramophone, Josephine suddenly recalled that her family had had one when she was growing up and that she used to sing along with it. How she loved music! The warm memories and sharing created such a loving atmosphere in the room that when the group had ended an hour later nobody seemed to want to move. Staff noticed that when we did return to the special care unit, the residents tended to sit together and to continue interacting.

QUALITIES OF FULL CIRCLE STAFF

Qualities of the Chaplain

- Capacity to be flexible and spontaneous—an ability to read/attend to what the group needs and adjust gracefully and quickly to that need
- Needs to be musical or at least musically sensitive—especially important, as not all music therapists are well-versed in the hymn repertoire
- Ability to work with story—recognizing that skill at the pulpit requires much more formal presentation—story is spontaneous and immediate—need to recognize the metaphorical aspects of story and understand how the subconscious processes them
- Need to be able to self-reflect and recognize deeper feelings about this particular population—to be in touch with your emotions

Qualities of the Music Therapist

- Must be aware of the form and structure music can offer the group—designing music intervention to engage the emotional and neurological realm of the participants
- Recognize the developmental implications of the geriatric phase —offering motivational aspects of music through the transitional period
- Willingness to see the potential wealth of living a lifetime, which is the unique contribution of each group participant

- Familiarity with church music and/or willingness to become familiar with the repertoire
- Ability to interpret "lyrical message" musically

Qualities of the Working Partnership

- Capacity to deal with the situation with immediacy
- Must respect and trust each other
- Ever mindful of the best interests of the group and how to facilitate that
- Leadership shared between partners
- Recognize the contributions each makes and affirm them
- Be open to learning from each other

A GUIDE TO USING THE THEMES

The songs provided in this book are suggestions only—ones that we have used whose content, or at least one verse, relates to the theme in question. The songs come from a wide range of faiths. If you have others in mind, please feel free to use them. In some cases, it is difficult to find the theme within the context of hymns, therefore, secular melodies are listed. Once again, draw upon your personal resources in selecting appropriate music. Hymns and secular songs that are familiar to your clientele will often be the most meaningful; using unfamiliar songs, however, can also focus their attention on the words. You might feel that you couldn't possibly learn all of these songs, so try learning one a week. If you don't have live music available, select two or three pieces from your CD collection. These themes can be used with high-functioning elderly. They can even be adapted for use with nonreligious groups by developing your own list of songs.

The stories, in most cases, are best told simply, in lay terms. As often as possible we tried to offer a biblical story or passage. Try to memorize the story or biblical passage, and tell it well: make eye contact with the group; use your voice dramatically. You may know other biblical passages or life stories relevant to the theme. Feel free to draw on other sources or personal experiences. You might even consider the telling of tales or myths, since they usually center on a common theme or moral. We also suggest telling the stories behind the hymns, where appropriate; good books are available on this subject, such as the Osbeck books cited in the bibliography.

The discussion time during sessions is for possible questions and ideas that might spark dialogue and reminiscing. Use your own judgment and sensitivity in drawing upon the questions offered here and in phrasing them. You don't need to ask all the questions, and you might have some better questions, based on the people in your group. Also, there is an art to asking questions: keep in mind your clientele and keep the questions concrete, simple, and affective. Maintain a limit to the number of questions so the discussion doesn't sound like a nosy inquisition. Sometimes one question is all it takes to create discussion within the group. Be open to exploring questions that may seem difficult or topics that are awkward to discuss. Think about how you would answer the questions. A group such as this must have a feeling of safety and trust to discuss some of the topics involved. Don't play "therapist" if you feel unable to handle the topic area and feelings that can and will arise. Allow the group time to think and respond. There are some blank pages at the end of the theme sections so you can create your own topics, songs, and questions.

Sensory cues add another dimension to the group—stimuli for the other senses. Be creative in the ways you stimulate and involve the group.

The prayers provided in this book are suggestions. You may want to create one each time, as we often did, relating it to specific people's needs in the group. Occasionally, a group member would lead us in prayer. If possible, join hands in prayer. If some do not want to hold hands, respect their boundaries. When praying, speak slowly and loudly enough for everyone to hear.

Working in the Moment

Always be willing to work with particular feelings and thoughts the group is expressing in the moment. Some days we would come to the group without any theme or agenda in mind, remaining open to the group's mood. Even if you have a theme planned and music prepared, the group may be in a completely different space. For example, they might be somber when the theme is "Joy." A principle of music therapy is to relate to the client and then change if necessary. You match the mood and feelings being presented through song, improvisation, creative expression, and dialogue, aiming for a positive change of mood and feelings, a resolution or shift in state of being. The same holds true for the pastoral care approach.

It takes practice and preparation to accommodate presenting emotions in the group. You need to have all hymns available to choose from and to be well-versed in them. You could also select a theme page that the group needs to explore and go with that. Try to determine how the group, as a whole, feels. You could ask them if they would like to explore a certain topic today, such as the one they're already talking about. This is especially useful with higher-functioning groups. You can then select or relate biblical passages pertinent to how the group is feeling—to the process that is unfolding.

With the special care elderly, this kind of group is not always effective because some days they are quiet. Such days are fine; they can involve gentle music, a biblical story, and a prayer about quietness. However, for the times when a concrete theme is needed, the absence of one can cause the group to stagnate because of lack of direction. Those with severe dementia seek structure, as provided through thematic discussion, related biblical passages, and music, which by its very nature is structural (rhythm, meter, melody).

The Setting

When *Full Circle* was formed, we had to take the members to a lounge that was located two floors above the special care unit. This meant coping with the elevator, which was scary for some participants. To borrow a phrase, "the difference was worth the distance." We discovered that the advantage of being in a comfortable, spacious, and pleasant setting compensated for the challenge of using the "lift." The lounge we used was carpeted, had comfortable furniture, and was tastefully decorated.

It is vital that the room has a door that can be closed to minimize the amount of external noise. If the group includes any "wanderers," it may be useful to have a door that locks. In the setting we were in, allowing the residents to wander out meant putting their safety at risk, since they could potentially walk out of the building undetected and become lost or gain access to the stairwells and fall.

The amount of external light also needs to be regulated. Strong sensory stimuli, either of the visual or auditory nature, should be avoided. Soft music and soft lighting are desirable. In general, the quality of the physical setting needs to express the conviction that the cognitively impaired are of great value, for example, comfortable furniture, plants, pictures, and pleasing decor.

The Sense and Composition of the Group

In a long-term care facility, there will be more people who can benefit from these groups than you can accommodate. Therefore, you will need to make decisions about the size and makeup of the group. We have found that for a leadership team of two the optimum number of residents is eight. On rare occasions, we have been a team of three (the additional person usually being a music therapy student) and have found that we can relate adequately to ten residents.

You should have at least two residents who normally are able to converse with the team. This creates a body of verbal interaction that is a bit like a water fountain from which others can be offered a drink. This may be partly our own need—to have those with whom we can have some lucid conversation. Whoever's need it is, that minimal conversational base seems to work best.

On the other hand, we can also cope with one person in the group whose conversation is unconnected—to our ears at least—with what is happening in the group or whose speech pattern is disruptive. This includes the perseverator, the anxious stutterer, as well as the person who seems to be on a different wavelength. However, having two such people in the group talking simultaneously subverts the group process.

We sometimes include "borderline" people who might also fit into a higher-achieving group. Since ours is a therapy situation, we can give needed one-on-one attention. This is true for those who take a long time to get their words out or who speak so softly that their words must be repeated for the rest of the group.

After several meetings, a sense of group seems to develop, evidenced by individuals showing less and less reluctance to come.

Once in the circle, they may drop clues that they recognize individuals or the setting. On one occasion, I asked a pleasant but confused person if she prayed. She responded, "in here"—which we assumed meant, "in this room where we customarily meet."

We have seen people accepted by the group who are used to being shouted at by other residents because they are noisy. One of the reasons is that we as group facilitators are (usually) able to model patience—the other residents in the group will follow our lead. Sometimes we follow their lead. One morning a resident was anxious, whimpering, and stuttering. The person next to her let me know several times that her neighbor was clearly unhappy. When I finally responded, she said, "I'm glad somebody else [besides herself] cares for her."

One deeply emotional experience is telling them when one of our group members dies. The reaction in our group is the same as in any other—shock, tension, and awe. Since unresolved loss is considered the biggest mental health problem among the cognitively impaired, it is a privilege to enable our small group to come to some resolution and repair.

On one occasion the group met just a few hours after a resident had died quite suddenly in his room. He had been a regular part of the group. The other residents didn't know but certainly must have sensed something had happened from the mood of the staff. We asked one member how she was doing, and she replied, "I was doing fine, then something happened . . . " We told the group about the man who had died and assisted them in their grieving and in understanding the losses associated with someone's death.

Our Religious "Bias"

It will be apparent that most of our music, scripture stories, and prayers are from the Christian tradition. There are two reasons for this: first, most long-term care residents who have a religious background are Christians. At the time of this writing, a smattering of other faiths was evident such as Buddhist, Sikh, and Jewish, and of course, some residents have no religious tradition. Sunday school attendance and churchgoing were the norm during the formative years of many of our residents. Hence, the Christian music heritage provides a significant point of contact with them.

Second, if a chaplain is involved in this program, the likelihood is that her or his religious background will include Christian music. A facility that has a music therapist who is familiar with religious music is highly favored.

Spirit-to-Spirit Connection

It is a constant struggle and challenge to understand the communication taking place in a group of the cognitively impaired. You observe the face and other parts of the body for clues. Sometimes you feel an "electricity" in the group, similar to what you experience with "normal" people. Often fragments of conversation have no obvious connection. At other times, surprisingly lucid recollections burst out.

This communication, which is ephemeral and seldom repeated, is constantly intriguing. It seems to be cognitive, and yet it has a super-cognitive dimension. One time, we had just completed a session in which death was the focus, and I was yet again grappling with the questions of what was really being understood. The music therapist, who is not from any particular religious persuasion, said, "When you talk about Jesus, about death, and about heaven, the attention of the group is galvanized." Thus, it seems as if something of cognitive worth "gets through."

How it happens is a mystery. *That* it happens, we are certain. When it happens, it comes as a complete surprise. Making it happen is out of the question. Being diligent, faithful, and alert seems to be our responsibility. We will see some results if we do not grow weary.

The Use of Touch

In a context in which verbal communication is "patchy," touch is one of our chief means of "speaking." We need to be conscious of the degree to which individuals are tactile—to respect the residents' ways of telling us that they need touch or that we should not invade their space. When residents are affectionate, we need to respond. A hug or a kiss on the cheek may not only be permissible but also crucial.

At the conclusion of our sessions, we try to facilitate the linking of hands with our neighbors. This, of course, is difficult, often impossible, with stroke-related weakness or constricted limbs. The possibility of social-physical contact and of deepening the sense of a caring spiritual community makes this an invaluable part of our routine.

During the singing of our closing song, we usually go around to each individual and offer the "right hand of fellowship" (a handshake). This provides the quiet, nonverbal residents with an opportunity to "say something." To a very modest degree, it also allows for the stretching of arm muscles and ligaments.

Holding a person's hand may produce some communication surprises. One resident may hold on, simply not wanting you to go away. Another may take your hand and touch it to her or his lips. Still another may squeeze your hand. Sometimes the cognitively impaired hang on to your hand, seemingly not knowing how to let go. We find it best in such instances not to forcefully extract our hands but to patiently and repetitively tell them that we need them to let us go.

The One and the Many: The Individual and the Group

One of the realities of any group is the tension that arises between the needs of the individuals and the needs of the group. Groups of cognitively impaired persons present this challenge in spades. Almost invariably, it is some form of speech that defines the challenge. Some individuals perseverate. Others' conversation seems to have no connection with what is being said in the group. There can be argumentative outbursts, sarcasm, crying, even wailing. Some stutter. Some speak so quietly that everything they say has to be repeated to keep the group involved. There may also be the impatient one who keeps saying, "Come on. Let's get going . . . " or "I want to go to bed," especially when the focus has shifted to someone else. This is one of the numerous reasons why two staff members are better than one—while one carries on with the group, the other can attend to particular individuals, offering explanation, reassurance, or, literally, hand-holding.

May we use gardening terms to illustrate what we have said thus far? We've talked about the traits and gifts the "gardeners" need.

We've mentioned the sequence of activities from preparing the soil to savoring the end results. We've described the climatic conditions that seem to work best and what to do when certain plants need special attention.

Now we want to display the tools that have worked well for us—the songs, stories, questions, visual and tactile aids. Our invitation to you now is to get to work. It's a process in which you will learn much. Like any good gardener you will have moments of sheer delight. You will also need patience to see the blossoming.

The "plants" are worth knowing and treasuring. You'll learn from them as they will be enriched by you. As the seasons unfold, you will have the joy of seeing them come full circle to comfort, humor, faith, and hope. May your enabling/gardening work bring them, and you, great joy.

NOTES

1. Canadian Association for Music Therapy brochure, "Music Therapy: A Health Care Profession," 1992.

2. Heriot, Cathy S. (1992). "Spirituality and aging," *Holistic Nursing Practice,* 7(1), p. 23. Material is this article appears in Ross Snyder, "In the aging years: Spirit," in C. LeFevre and P. LeFevre (Eds.), *Aging and the Human Spirit: A Reader in Religion and Gerontology,* Second Edition, pp. 83-85. ©1981 by the Exploration Press, a division of Chicago Theological Seminary. Used by permission.

3. Koenig, Harold G. (1990). "Research on religion and mental health in later life: A review and commentary," *Journal of Geriatric Psychiatry* 23(1), p. 33.

4. Nikles, Robin (1992). "Integration of music therapy and theology: A preliminary approach," *The Australian Journal of Music Therapy,* 3, p. 53.

5. Heriot, "Spirituality and aging," p. 29.

6. Ibid., p. 26.

7. Nikles, "Integration of music therapy and theology," p. 53.

THEMES

Feelings

ANGER

Hymns About Anger

Battle Hymn of the Republic
Fight the Good Fight, with All Thy Might
Lord, Rebuke Me Not in Anger
Love Lifted Me (verse 3)
My Anchor Holds
Will Your Anchor Hold? (We Have An Anchor)

Hymns to Soothe Anger

Be Thou My Vision
He
Help Us Accept Each Other
There'll Be Peace in the Valley
There's a Quiet Understanding

Secular Songs

Angry (Please Don't Be Angry)

Story

The Cleansing of the Temple—Mark 11:15-17

Quotations

1. Psalm 139, especially verses 19-22
2. Psalm 4:4-5
3. Let not the sun go down upon your wrath.

Ephesians 4:26 (KJV)

4. A soft answer turneth away wrath: but grievous words stir up anger.

Proverbs 15:1 (KJV)

19

5. Let all bitterness, and wrath, and anger, and clamour, and evil speaking, be put away from you, with all malice: And be ye kind one to another, tender-hearted, forgiving one another, even as God for Christ's sake hath forgiven you.

Ephesians 4:31-32 (KJV)

Discussion

1. Have you ever been angry? What happened?
2. When was the last time you got really angry? What was it about?
3. Does it still make you angry to think about it now?
4. How do you express your anger? Does the anger burn slowly or erupt?
5. Did your father (mother, spouse) ever get angry with you (or vice versa)?
6. Is it okay to get angry?
7. The Bible says, "Let not the sun go down upon your wrath": What does that mean to you?
8. What happens if we have anger but don't express it?
9. Did Jesus ever get angry? Why?
10. How can we learn from His example?

Sensory Cue

Pass around a picture of a thunder and lightning storm.

Prayer

Lord God, help us to be honest about our anger; help us to express our anger in healthy ways. Sometimes we don't want others to be angry—especially when they're angry at us. Help us and others to express our anger with honesty and understanding, following Jesus' example. We ask this in His Name. Amen.

H. McIlveen

Note

Comment on how we sometimes say it is "an angry sky." Use this as a bridge to introducing the theme.

CONFIDENCE

Hymns

Arise, My Soul, Arise (especially verse 5)
Awake, My Soul, and with the Sun
Be Not Afraid
Be Still, My Soul (verse 2)
Blessed Assurance, Jesus Is Mine
Dare to Be a Daniel
He's Got the Whole World in His Hands
I Am Trusting Thee, Lord Jesus
It Is Well with My Soul
Jesus Lives and So Shall I
Jesus, Thy Blood and Righteousness
My Lord Knows the Way
Never Give Up
O, for a Faith That Will Not Shrink
On the Victory Side
Savior, Like a Shepherd Lead Us
Stand Up, Stand Up for Jesus
Take the Name of Jesus with You
Trust and Obey
Wonderful Jesus (especially verse 5)

Secular Songs

Anything You Can Do (I Can Do Better)
Climb Every Mountain (from *The Sound of Music*)
I Am Woman (Helen Reddy)
I Did It My Way (Frank Sinatra)
I Have Confidence (from *The Sound of Music*)
The Impossible Dream
Whistle a Happy Tune (from *The King and I*)
You'll Never Walk Alone (from *Carousel*)

Stories

1. David kills Goliath—I Samuel 17
2. Mark 5:25-34

Quotations

1. In quietness and confidence shall be your strength.

   Isaiah 30:15 (NKJV)

2. I can do all things through Christ which strengtheneth me.

   Philippians 4:13 (KJV)

3. When thou passest through the waters, I will be with thee; and through the rivers, they shall not overflow thee: when thou walkest through the fire, thou shalt not be burned; neither shall the flame kindle upon thee.

   Isaiah 43:2 (KJV)

   (Note: This quotation goes well with the hymn "Be Not Afraid.")

Discussion

1. If you could get close enough to Jesus to touch him, what might happen to you? What would you like to have happen to you?
2. How did the woman in the story know that she was healed? What was different?
3. How can you tell if someone is self-confident?
4. Would you say you're a confident person? Are you self-confident?
5. What are you confident about? (You might suggest an attribute or personal success of the resident, such as career, sense of humor, cooking, knowledge, insight.)
6. Would you say you lack confidence?
7. What kinds of things give us confidence (success, love, praise)?
8. Does God's love give you confidence?

Sensory Cue

Demonstrate how a confident person looks—head held high, erect posture, proud face.

Prayer

Teach us, good Lord, to serve you as you deserve; to give and not to count the cost; to fight and not to heed the wounds; to toil and not to seek for rest; to labor and not to ask for any reward, except that of knowing that we do your will; through Jesus Christ Our Lord.

Ignatius of Loyola, Prayer for Generosity

CONFUSION

Hymns

Be Thou My Vision
I Heard the Voice of Jesus Say
Just As I Am, Without One Plea
Lord, I Was Blind
May the Mind of Christ My Savior
Open My Eyes, That I May See
Where Cross the Crowded Ways of Life

Secular Songs

Alfie
Ball of Confusion (That's What This World Is)
Bewitched, Bothered, and Bewildered (from the movie *Pal Joey*)
Crazy World (from the movie *Victor/Victoria*)
Do You Know Where You're Going To? (theme from *Mahogany*)
What'll I Do?

Story

The book of Job, Chapters 1 and 2

Quotation

> For where envying and strife is, there is confusion and every evil work. But the wisdom that is from above is first pure, then peaceable, gentle, and easy to be entreated, full of mercy and good fruits, without partiality, and without hypocrisy. And the fruit of righteousness is sown in peace of them that make peace.
>
> *James 3:16-18 (KJV)*

Discussion

1. If you feel confused, how can I help you?
2. Does peaceful friendship (and music) make the confusion go away?

3. What is the worst type of confusion? What is it like?
4. What is one thing that will never change (within the person and/or without)?

Sensory Cue

The use of a simple, peaceful song may help focus and relax: "Be Still and Know That I Am God," "Kum By Ya," or a gentle "Alleluia" song.

Prayer

God, we pray for those with disturbed and troubled thoughts—for those who have lost their bearings. Be to them light in their darkness, comfort in their fear. Above all may they sense that You, who bear all our sufferings, understand them. Through Christ we pray.

H. McIlveen

DEPRESSION

Hymns

Abide with Me
Be Still, My Soul
Hark, My Soul, It Is the Lord (written by William Cowper, who had
    severe mental illness)
His Eye Is on the Sparrow
How Sweet the Name of Jesus Sounds
Love Lifted Me
Put on the Garment of Praise for the Spirit of Heaviness
The Servant Song

Secular songs

Alfie
Am I Blue?
Smile the While
Vincent (Don McLean)
Without You (Harry Nilsson)
Yesterday

Stories

1. The story of Elijah's depression—I Kings 19:1-18
2. The story of the life of hymn writer William Cowper (Stern-Owens, 1993, pp. 32-35)
3. The story of Charlotte Elliott, who wrote "Just as I Am" (Osbeck, 1982, pp. 146-147)

Quotation

> For lo, the winter is past, the rain is over and gone; the flowers appear on the earth; the time of the singing of birds is come, and the voice of the turtle is heard in our land.

> *Song of Solomon 2:11-12 (KJV)*

Discussion

1. Demonstrate bodily postures that might be shown by someone who is depressed.
2. Have you ever felt depressed? Have you ever gone through a period of depression?
3. What is it like when you feel down or blue?
4. Did you ever feel so depressed that you wanted to die? Is it all right to tell God that you want to die?
5. What might He do for us? It may be helpful to say what He did for Elijah: physical care, a walk in nature, reassurances that others are with us and that we are still needed.
6. Was there a time in your life when you felt depressed?
7. What's it like to be depressed? Are you depressed now?
8. What helps when someone is feeling down? How can we help each other?
9. Who do you turn to when you're feeling down?

Sensory Cue

Use paintings by Edvard Munch or Vincent van Gogh.

Prayer

Lord Jesus Christ, light shining in our darkness, have mercy on our tired and doubting hearts. Renew in us the courage we need. Amen.

A Prayer from the Taize Community in France

ENCOURAGEMENT AND SUPPORT

Hymns

The core message of many hymns is about support. The following are some of the many hymns that carry this message.

Abba Father
Be Thou My Vision
Be with Me
Because He Lives
Blessed Assurance, Jesus Is Mine
God of Grace and God of Glory
God Will Take Care of You
He Leadeth Me, O Blessed Thought
His Eye Is on the Sparrow
I Heard the Voice of Jesus Say
I Will Never Forget You
It Is Well with My Soul
Jesus Is All I Need
Jesus, Lover of My Soul
Just as I Am, Without One Plea
Keep Me from Sinking Down
Lead, Kindly Light
Leaning on the Everlasting Arms
Like Cedars They Shall Stand
Morning Has Broken
My God, My Father, Make Me Strong
Nearer, My God, to Thee
Never Give Up
Nobody Knows the Trouble I've Seen
Remember All the People
Softly and Tenderly Jesus Is Calling
Somebody Cares for Me
The Servant Song
This Day God Gives Me
Turn Your Eyes upon Jesus
What a Friend We Have in Jesus

Secular Songs

Flying on Your Own (Rita MacNeil)
Keep Right on to the End of the Road
Stand by Me
There's a Bluebird on Your Windowsill
You'll Never Walk Alone
You've Got a Friend

Story

Barnabas (whose name means "son of encouragement") helps Saul of Tarsus—Acts 4:36-37

Discussion

1. Who has encouraged you in life?
2. Did your parents encourage you? How did they do this? If not, how did that feel?
3. Was/Is your wife/husband/partner encouraging and supportive?
4. Do you feel supported/encouraged by God?
5. Do you encourage or support others (friends, relatives, children)?
6. Do you feel support in your life now?

Sensory Cue

Ask a member of the group to support the music being used by playing an instrument with a good solid beat, such as a drum or similar percussion instrument. Use music with a steady beat, such as "He Leadeth Me," "What a Friend We Have in Jesus," or "Leaning on the Everlasting Arms."

Prayers

1. O God, Our Father, let us not be content to wait and see what will happen, but give us the determination to make the right things happen. While time is running out, save us from patience

which is akin to cowardice. Give us the courage to be either hot or cold, to stand for something, lest we fall for anything. In Jesus' name, Amen.

Peter Marshall
The Hodder Book of Christian Prayers
(Castle, 1986, p. 283)

2. See a Jewish prayer for healing (#839) in *The Oxford Book of Prayer* (Appleton, 1985, p. 276).

ENVY AND JEALOUSY

Hymns

Come Let Us Sing of a Wonderful Love (verse 4)
He Is Our Peace Who Has Broken Down Every Wall
May the Mind of Christ My Savior
O Love That Will Not Let Me Go
Prayer of St. Francis (Make Me a Channel of Your Peace)
The Servant Song
This Is My Commandment
Though the Fig Tree Does Not Blossom

Secular Songs

Jalousie
Jealous

Stories

1. The story of the relationship between King Saul and David is a rich example of the nature and power of jealousy—I Samuel 18:1-16
2. Tell the story of Hera (the Romans called her Juno) who was characterized as extremely envious. The wife of Zeus, she punished any woman he fell in love with. "She never forgot an injury" (Hamilton, 1942, p. 27). On another occasion a Trojan remarked how another goddess was lovelier than Hera. Her jealousy resulted in the continuation of the Trojan War and the eventual destruction of the city of Troy.

Discussion

1. What does it mean when someone is "green with envy"?
2. Have you ever been "green with envy"? Do you remember the occasion?
3. Were you ever jealous of somebody else?
4. Has anyone been jealous of you? Why?

5. Was/Is your husband/wife ever jealous?
6. Is it wrong to be envious of someone else?

Sensory Cue

Demonstrate facially how we pout over what someone else has or what a "jealous" look is like, or bring a picture of someone looking clearly envious of the other. When used in context a pout or a squinted eye should help convey the feeling.

Prayer

> In me there is darkness
> But with You there is light,
> I am lonely, but you leave me not.
> I am restless, but with You there is peace.
> In me there is bitterness, but with You there is patience;
> Your ways are past understanding, but
> You know the way for me.

Dietrich Bonhoeffer
The Hodder Book of Christian Prayers
(Castle, 1986, p. 153)

FAITH

Hymns

Alleluia, Sing to Jesus
Authors of Faith
Faith Is the Victory
Faith of Our Fathers
Great Is Thy Faithfulness
He Touched Me
Jesus Is All the World to Me
My Faith Has Found a Resting Place
My Faith Looks up to Thee
O, for a Faith That Will Not Shrink
Over My Head
Standing on the Promises
Trust and Obey

Secular Songs

Climb Every Mountain
I Believe

Story

The healing of a boy with an evil spirit—Mark 9:14-29

Discussion

1. Do you believe the biblical phrase, "Everything is possible for the person who has faith"?
2. Have you ever had faith in something happening and it did?
3. The father in the story believed in Christ a little bit, but not a lot. Do you sometimes just have a *little* faith? How could our faith grow?
4. Do you believe that Jesus can love you/help you/touch you right now?

Sensory Cues

1. Show pictures of different religious groups involved in the celebration of their faiths.
2. It may also be appropriate to recite the Apostles' Creed or the Nicene Creed.

Prayer

> Behold, Lord, an empty vessel that needs to be filled.
> My Lord; fill it.
> I am weak in the faith; strengthen me.
> I do not have a strong and firm faith; at times I doubt
> and am unable to trust you altogether.
> O Lord, help me. Strengthen my faith and trust in you.

Martin Luther
The Hodder Book of Christian Prayers
(Castle, 1986, p. 148)

FEAR

Hymns

All the Way My Savior Leads Me
Alone with None but Thee (verse 1)
Amazing Grace
Be Not Afraid
Because He Lives
Blest Be the Lord
Dare to Be a Daniel
Do Not Be Afraid
Give to the Winds Your Fears
God of Grace and God of Glory
Standing by a Purpose True
Tell It to Jesus (verse 3)
What Time I Am Afraid
Will Your Anchor Hold? (We Have an Anchor) (verse 2)

Secular Songs

Hero (Mariah Carey)
I Whistle a Happy Tune
Who's Afraid of the Big Bad Wolf?
You'll Never Walk Alone

Story

Jesus calms a storm at sea—Luke 8:22-25

Quotations

1. Psalm 23, especially verse 4
2. Be not afraid, neither be thou dismayed: for the Lord thy God is with thee whithersoever thou goest.

Joshua 1:9 (KJV)

Discussion

1. Have you ever been afraid? What of?
2. Are you ever scared of something? What do you do when you're scared or afraid? What helps? Who helps?

3. When you are afraid, who would you run to?
4. Ask the group to show how we look/act when we are afraid—if helpful, demonstrate cringing, nail biting, even hiding behind a chair.

Sensory Cue

Light a candle in the center of the circle.

Prayer

Teach us, O Lord, to fear without being afraid; to fear you in love that we may love You without fear; through Jesus Christ our Lord.

Christina Rossetti
The Hodder Book of Christian Prayers
(Castle, 1986, p. 159)

FORGIVENESS

Hymns

Amazing Grace
An Evening Prayer ("If I have wounded . . . ")
Arise, My Soul, Arise (verse 3)
Come, Let Us Reason Together
Dear Lord, Forgive
Glory to Thee My God (verse 2)
Grace and Truth Shall Mark the Way
Happy Day
Heal Me, Hands of Jesus (verse 2)
Help Us Accept Each Other
I Then Shall Live
I Will Sweep Away Your Transgressions
Jesus Forgives and Forgets
Jesus Is Passing This Way
Jesus, Keep Me Near the Cross
Just as I Am, Without One Plea
Kind and Merciful God (verse 4)
Out of the Depths I Cry
Pass Me Not
Prayer of St. Francis (Make Me a Channel of Your Peace)
Redeemed, Restored, Forgiven
Rock of Ages, Cleft for Me
What a Friend We Have in Jesus

Secular Songs

Don't Wait Too Long to Forgive
Forgiveness
He
The Living Years (Mike and the Mechanics)

Stories

1. *Edith Cavell's death and affirmation.* Edith Cavell (1865-1915) was an English nurse, first matron of a Red Cross hospital in

Brussels, Belgium, during World War I. She assisted about 200 English, Belgian, and French soldiers to escape to Holland between November 1914 and July 1915. She was arrested by the Germans, condemned to death by court-martial, and shot along with a Belgian who had provided guides (*Merriam-Webster's Biographical Dictionary*, 1995, p. 192). Her last words before her execution on October 12, 1915 were: "I realize that patriotism is not enough. I must have no hatred or bitterness towards anyone" (Bartlett, 1992, p. 590).
2. The death of Canadian Governor General Georges Vanier, Charles Lynch's "part" in that death, and Madame Vanier's response. (See Lynch, 1983.)
3. *Les Misérables* by Victor Hugo is a powerful story about forgiveness.

Discussion

1. What is the worst thing that stains clothes (grape juice, mud)?
2. What is the worst thing someone might do? (Examples group members have cited include: betray a friend, commit murder, destroy pretty things, kill a child, tell a lie, steal money.)
3. What is the worst thing you have done? Could God forgive that? If yes, how? If not, why?
4. Have you ever been angry at someone and stayed angry? Did you ever make up? Were you able to forgive?
5. Some people say to "forgive and forget." Is that possible? Have you ever done that?
6. Recite The Lord's Prayer together and discuss the part: "forgive us our trespasses as we forgive those who trespass against us."

Sensory Cue

Use a chalkboard or other erasable board to list acts the group would like forgiveness for or would like to forgive someone for, then erase it when the list is complete. Or, do this person by person, each time erasing the word. Either at the conclusion or with each word, say "That's what forgiveness is like."

Prayer

O Lord, because we often sin and have to ask for pardon, help us to forgive as we would be forgiven; neither mentioning old offenses committed against us, nor dwelling upon them in thought; but loving our sister/brother freely as you freely love us; for Your name's sake.

Christina Rossetti
The Hodder Book of Christian Prayers
(Castle, 1986, p. 72)

FREEDOM

Hymns

Approach, My Soul, the Mercy Seat
Free at Last
Freedom
How Firm a Foundation
Jesus Loves Even Me
On the Wings of a Snow White Dove
Steal Away, Steal Away Home
Thou Art My Vision

Secular Songs

Abraham, Martin, and John
Born Free
Don't Fence Me In
Escape (Janet Jackson)
Happy Wanderer
I Wish I Knew How It Would Feel to Be Free

Story

Jacob, running away from his brother—Genesis 27

Quotations

1. And I said, Oh that I had wings like a dove! for then would I fly away, and be at rest. Lo, then would I wander far off, and remain in the wilderness.

Psalm 55:6-7 (KJV)

2. Our soul is escaped as a bird out of the snare of the fowlers:
The snare is broken and we are escaped.
Our help is in the name of the Lord,
Who made heaven and earth.

Psalm 124:7, 8 (KJV)

Discussion

1. Do you ever feel cooped up?
2. Where might you go if you had the "wings of a dove"?
3. Did you ever run away from home? Why? Would you like to run away now?
4. If you could run off for a few days, where would you go? With whom would you escape? What would you do?
5. Discuss how some people escape from dealing with their problems by turning to alcohol, food, sleep, etc.

Sensory Cue

Pass a skeleton key around the group and see what associations it evokes. Ask what it might be used for, such as unlocking a door.

Prayer

O God our Father, hear me, who am trembling in this darkness, and stretch forth your hand to me; hold your light forth before me; recall me from my wanderings and be my Guide.

St. Augustine of Hippo
The Hodder Book of Christian Prayers
(Castle, 1986, p. 243)

Note

Escaping can be a meaningful theme for the institutionalized elderly, especially those who are on a locked or secured unit. The desire to get out of the environment they're in, to be outdoors, to be free to come and go is strong. These are needs that not only need to be acknowledged; they need to be met. Therefore, hosting this kind of group is better in a location other than the unit they live on.

JOY

Hymns

Blessed Assurance, Jesus Is Mine
Bringing in the Sheaves
Cry Out with Joy
I Come with Joy to Meet My Lord
I Have the Joy, Joy, Joy
I Was Full of Joy
Joyful, Joyful, We Adore Thee
Joy Is Like the Rain
Joy to the World! The Lord Is Come
Joy Unspeakable
Leaning on the Everlasting Arms
The Ninety and Nine
O Love That Will Not Let Me Go (verse 2)
O That Will Be Glory (verse 3)
Rejoice, Ye Pure in Heart
Whosoever Will

Secular Songs

Ain't We Got Fun?
Blue Skies
Enjoy Yourself, It's Later Than You Think
Get Happy
Hava Nagilah
Joy to the World (Three Dog Night)
Put on a Happy Face

Stories

1. The angel tells the shepherds about the birth of Christ—Luke 2:8-12
2. Discuss the stories of the lost sheep, pieces of silver, or the two sons—Luke 15:1-7

Poem

"She Loved to Laugh," author unknown.

> She loved to laugh, and some way, she
> Woke others to a sense of glee,
> And many found, when she was near,
> An unaccustomed note of cheer
> In everything they heard, or saw;
> It seemed some undiscovered law,
> Which made dull things of every day,
> Reflect her bearing, blithe and gay!
>
> She loved to laugh, and when she came,
> A flicker, as of happy flame,
> Sprang swiftly up, re-echoing,
> As one bird's song makes others sing.
> O, laughter is a blessed gift,
> Heals many a hurt, mends many a rift;
> She loved to laugh, and so she lent
> to other lives her merriment.

Edward MacHugh's Treasury
of Gospel Hymns and Poems, 1938

Discussion

1. What brought you joy in life?
2. What *brings* you joy in your life today?
3. Do you remember an event that brought you joy? (You may need to cue them about specific events such as marriage, having children, getting a job, going on a special holiday, being reunited with family.)

Sensory Cue

Sometimes laughter brings great joy. We have a wonderfully silly device called a laughing box. When you push the button, a recording of someone laughing hysterically starts playing, which is so infectious that everyone starts chuckling. Give it to one of the residents and ask her or him if they know what it is, what it might be for, and "Is there a button to push?" It's much more fun if they discover it's use and function for themselves.

Prayer

Lord, you have sent me joy! I leap . . . I skip . . . it is good to be alive. You give life; you give the spirit of gladness to feed it. I love you. My sins are forgiven. It is good to be alive . . . and you have made it so.

Hubert van Zeller, OSB
The Hodder Book of Christian Prayers
(Castle, 1986, p. 253)

Note

You can also sing lively, joyful songs, such as "He's Got the Whole World in His Hands," "Put Your Hand in the Hand," etc. Encourage the residents to clap along with the beat and to sing out.

MEMORIES AND MEMORIES LOST

Hymns

Awake, O Israel (verse 2)
Can a Little Child Like Me?
Count Your Blessings
Do Lord, Remember Me (verse 2)
Here, Where Memories Gather
I Will Never Forget You
Jesus Loves Even Me (verse 2)
Just as I Am, Without One Plea
Precious Memories
Remember All the People
These Remind Me of God
This Is a Time to Remember
When the World Forgets You (He Remembers You)

Also, hymns that the group members may have learned as children or hymns that bring back memories of certain occasions.

Secular Songs

As Time Goes By
Do You Remember?
I Remember It Well
If I Forget You
Lead Me Home
Memories
Precious Memories (Lonnie Combs and J. B. Wright)
Try to Remember
The Way We Were
When I Grow Too Old to Dream

Story

The hymn "I Will Never Forget You" is based on this passage from Isaiah 49:15-16 (NIV): "Can a mother forget the baby at her breast and have no compassion on the child she has borne? Though she may forget, I will not forget you! See, I have engraved you in the palm of my hands . . . "

Quotation

> Then those who feared the Lord spoke with one another; the Lord heeded and heard them, and a book of remembrance was written before him of those who thought about Him.
>
> *Malachi 3:16 (KJV)*

Poem

"Remembrance," author unknown.

> I want you to know you are never forgotten,
> that the old, old days hid in memory sweet
> are still a part of my life that I cherish
> without them so much would be incomplete.
> And you are mixed up with so much I remember,
> your name so often I utter in prayer,
> never forgotten, on earth, or in heaven,
> always the child of God's tenderest care.
>
> I want you to know you are never forgotten;
> that my thoughts and my prayers are folding you round—
> rest in His promises, go where He sends you,
> do what He bids you, faithful be found.
> Look up and trust Him, a new day is dawning,
> stretch out your hand and take His today;
> bought by Him, loved by Him; never forgotten,
> his in His heart forever and aye.
>
> *Edward MacHugh's Treasury*
> *of Gospel Hymns and Poems, 1938*

Discussion

1. Does your memory ever let you down? (Some might say no.)
2. Does it bother you that sometimes you can't remember something?

3. Validate the frustration they might feel concerning their memory loss.
4. Give them opportunities to talk about how it feels, what it's like.
5. Even if we sometimes forget things, who always remembers us (family, friends, God, Jesus)?—use hymns such as "I Will Never Forget You" here.
6. What are some of your most precious memories (you might have to cue them based on your knowledge of their past): special holiday, getting married, buying a house, having a baby, falling in love, etc.
7. Can you think of a memory that makes you laugh?
8. Can you think of a memory that makes you cry?
9. Can you think of a memory that makes you angry?
10. Can you recall a romantic memory?
11. What can we use to help our memory? A wedding ring? A string on the finger? A picture? A picture or icon of Jesus?
12. Do you think God ever forgets us? (Then refer to one of the verses above.)

Sensory Cues

1. Photographs or mementos (a locket with a picture of someone that can be worn around the neck and close to the heart might help convey the idea of God not forgetting, by keeping us close). Personal articles that the group has which they can reminisce about. Be sure to ask them if it's okay to bring one or two of their personal items along to the group. If possible, select the items with the person.
2. Create a book of remembrance for each of the group members, including familiar photos, memorabilia, pictures of favorite places, favorite songs, and poems.

Prayers

1. Lord Jesus Christ, take all my freedom, my memory, my understanding, and my will. All that I have and cherish, you have given me. I surrender it all to be guided by your will. Your grace

and your love are wealth enough for me. Give me these, Lord Jesus, and I ask for nothing more.

Ignatius of Loyola
The Hodder Book of Christian Prayers
(Castle, 1986, p. 93)

2. The prayer of the thief on the Cross: "Lord, remember me when you come into your kingdom." Jesus replied: "Today you shall be with me in paradise." Lord, we thank you for the memories that we have. We thank you that, although others may forget us, you keep us in your book of remembrance, you engrave us on the palm of your hand. You remember us even when we forget you. Thank you. Amen.

H. McIlveen

Notes

Be sure to convey the message that group members are loved no matter what; they are loved for who they are. The awareness that they have memory loss and have declined in health may be present. This can create low self-esteem and low self-worth and feelings of being a nuisance, of wanting to die. Use the hymn "Just as I Am, Without One Plea" to reinforce that they are loved no matter what, loved just as they are—by the group, by you as facilitators, and by God.

You might also ask if they went to Sunday school and what they remember about it. Sing hymns they may have sung then.

ORPHANED/LONELY/ABANDONED

Hymns

If appropriate and for purposes of closure and healing, end with songs about love, support, and friendship.

Be Not Afraid
I Will Never Forget You
I'll Walk Beside You
O Love That Will Not Let Me Go
Sometimes I Feel Like a Motherless Child
What a Friend We Have in Jesus

Secular Songs

All Alone
All By Myself
Among My Souvenirs
Are You Lonesome Tonight?
Eleanor Rigby
I Know What It Means to Be Lonesome
I'm So Lonesome I Could Cry
Only the Lonely (Roy Orbison)
She Wore a Yellow Ribbon
Tie a Yellow Ribbon ('Round the Old Oak Tree)
You'll Never Walk Alone (from *Carousel*)

Quotations

1. My God, my God, why hast Thou forsaken me?

    Matthew 27:46 (KJV)

2. Though my father and mother forsake me, the Lord will receive me.

    Psalm 27:10 (NIV)

Story

The story behind "O Love That Will Not Let Me Go" (Osbeck, 1982, pp. 189-190)

Discussion

1. Do you remember *Little Orphan Annie,* the cartoon?
2. Did anyone here grow up as an orphan? Were you adopted?
3. Were there moments in your life when you felt abandoned or lonely?
4. Psalm 71:9 says, "Don't cast me off in the time of old age; don't forsake me when my strength fails." Do you ever feel that way now?
5. Have you ever felt like you're all alone in the world?
6. Do you sense God's (or Jesus') presence when you feel most alone? Does that help?
7. Has God helped you through times of loneliness?
8. Do you think about your parents and wish they (or one of them) were here now? What would that be like?

Sensory Cues

1. Bring along a cartoon clip of *Little Orphan Annie.* Pass it around the group. Elicit comments and memories.
2. Pass a yellow ribbon tied in a knot around the group and discuss it in the context of the yellow ribbon songs—how a yellow ribbon symbolizes waiting for a loved one you miss.

Prayers

1. Let the cry of widows, orphans and destitute children enter into Your ears, O most loving Savior. Comfort them with a mother's tenderness, shield them from the perils of the world, and bring them at last to Your heavenly home.

   John Cosin
   The Hodder Book of Christian Prayers
   (Castle, 1986, p. 236)

2. You who said, "I will never leave you or forsake you," help us to know deeply that even if our mother and father forsake us, You will take us up. Through your mercy we pray. Amen.

   H. McIlveen

Note

Some institutionalized elderly think/feel they've been orphaned because they've regressed to childhood; they feel lost and seek the comfort they once knew with their parents. They may also feel abandoned by family because they do no live at home and often forget that family is actually visiting regularly. Unfortunately, there are some who don't have family or whose family does not visit. This theme may need to be explored over several sessions.

RECONCILIATION

Hymns

Arise, My Soul, Arise
Because He Died and Is Risen (verse 2)
Bind Us Together
Christ Has for Sin Atonement Made
Come Back to Me
Father, I Have Sinned
Forgive Our Sins As We Forgive
He
He Is Our Peace
Help Us Accept Each Other
I Will Sweep Away Your Transgressions
In Christ There Is No East or West
Jesus Comes with All His Grace (especially verse 3)
Just as I Am, Without One Plea
Lord, I'm Coming Home
On Jordan's Stormy Banks I Stand
Peace Prayer
Prayer of St. Francis (Make Me a Channel of Your Peace)
The Prodigal Son
Though the Mountains May Fall
We Are One in the Bond of Love
What a Wonderful Savior
Wonderful Jesus

Secular Songs

Come Back to Sorrento
Day by Day (from *Godspell*)
Don't Wait Too Long to Forgive
Forgiveness
I'm Sorry I Made You Cry
The Living Years (Mike and the Mechanics)
Return to Me
That's What Friends Are For
Why (Annie Lennox)

Story

The Prodigal Son—Luke 15

Discussion

1. Did you ever have a fight with someone and then reconcile your differences? Who was it? Do you remember what it was over? Who made the first gesture of reconciliation?
2. What about today—is there anyone in your life with whom you would like to reconcile? Do you feel reconciled with God?

Sensory Cue

Show a picture of two people embracing and reuniting or perhaps of two important world leaders shaking hands over a peace treaty.

Prayer

The Lord's Prayer—especially the petition "Forgive us our trespasses as we forgive those who trespass against us."

Note

Some people have difficulty feeling reconciled with God and hold on to their guilt and fears about sin. There are many who have not reconciled differences with family members, information for which you may need to consult their social history. Be prepared to follow up on the beginning steps of reconciliation. For some family members, the pain of having their loved one not recognize them is too difficult to face. You may be able to facilitate contact. Feelings of guilt and loss after their loved one dies weigh heavier than dealing with those feelings when that person is alive.

SHAME

Hymns

Ah, What Shame I Have to Bear
Beneath the Cross of Jesus (verse 3)
Hallelujah! What a Savior (verse 2)
He Touched Me
I Am Not Worthy
Now I Belong to Jesus (verse 2)
O the Bitter Shame and Sorrow
The Old Rugged Cross
What a Friend We Have in Jesus

Secular Songs

Hang Your Head in Shame (Red Foley)
Help Me Understand (Hank and Audrey Williams)
The Picture Turned Toward the Wall
Shame (Elton Britt)
Shame, Shame, Brazen Little Raisin
Walkin' the Sidewalks of Shame (Jimmy Wakely)

Stories

1. Parable of the Pharisee and the tax collector—Luke 18:9-14
2. Jesus' shame—Matthew 27:27-31

Discussion

1. "Shame on you"—what does that sentence bring to mind? When do we say that?
2. What does the feeling "shame" mean? Have you ever experienced it? What helps to feel better?
3. Do you remember feeling shamed (or ashamed)?
4. Is there anything you still feel ashamed about now that you've done in the past?
5. Does guilt accompany shame?

Sensory Cue

Demonstrate the bodily postures associated with being ashamed—head hung down, your hands covering your face, stooped posture, cowering in a corner.

Prayers

1. Use verse 3 of "Beneath the Cross of Jesus":

   I take, O cross, thy shadow for my abiding place;
   I ask no other sunshine than the sunshine of His face,
   Content to let the world go by, to know no gain nor loss,
   My sinful self my only shame, My glory all the cross.

   Giesbrecht, 1973, p. 86

2. Lord when I can't look You or other people in the face, let me feel your gentle hand lifting my chin so that I can look into Your eyes and know Your acceptance. Thank you for taking our shame upon You and lifting us up. For Your name's sake, Amen.

   H. McIlveen

SORROW/GRIEF

Hymns

Abide with Me
Be Not Afraid (verse 3)
Children of the Heavenly Father (verse 3)
Come, Ye Disconsolate, Where'er Ye Languish
Cross of Jesus, Cross of Sorrow
Hallelujah! What a Savior
If You Will Trust in God to Guide You (verse 2)
It Is Well with My Soul
Kum By Yah
No Other Plea
O Sacred Head, Now Wounded
Thank You for Giving Me the Morning (verse 2)
There Is a Balm in Gilead
Through the Love of God our Savior
Through the Night of Doubt and Sorrow
Trust and Obey (verse 2)
Were You There When They Crucified My Lord?
What a Friend We Have in Jesus
When We Walk with the Lord

Secular Songs

Crying (Roy Orbison and Joe Melson)
Tears in Heaven (Eric Clapton)
Without You (Harry Nilsson)

Stories

1. Jesus encountering the grief of Mary and Martha when their brother died—John 11:17-37, especially verse 35, "Jesus wept."
2. The stories behind "It Is Well with My Soul," "O Love that Will Not Let Me Go," or "The Ninety and Nine. (Sources for these stories may be found in Osbeck, 1982, pp. 126, 189, and 250.)

Quotation

> Alone, dear Lord, ah, yes! alone with Thee!
> My aching heart at rest, my spirit free;
> My sorrow gone, my burdens all forgotten,
> When far away I soar alone with Thee.

Oswald J. Smith

Discussion

1. How can we tell when someone is sad?
2. What are the body signals which tell that they are sad?
3. What has been your greatest loss? Your greatest sorrow?
4. What do you do when you feel grief? How do you cope?
5. Do you ever get over the loss of a loved one?
6. What can we do to help those in mourning—Hold them? Cry with them? Sing together? Just be present?
7. How would you like others to comfort you?

Sensory Cues

1. A handkerchief or tissue to wipe the eyes and tears
2. Edvard Munch's painting *The Sickroom*

Prayer

> Almighty God, Father of mercies and giver of all comfort; deal graciously, we pray, with all those who mourn, that, casting every care on You, they may know the consolation of Your love; through Jesus Christ our Lord.

Book of Common Prayer

Note

Sometimes it's a personally meaningful song that evokes someone's sorrow and grief. Perhaps it's their favorite song or a song that reminds them of someone they miss or have lost. Even a song that seems cheerful to one person may be the song that touches the heart of another.

TOGETHERNESS AND UNITY

Hymns

Bind Us Together Lord
Blest Be the Tie that Binds
God and Man at Table Are Sat Down
Help Us Accept Each Other
He's Got the Whole World in His Hands
The Ninety and Nine
Now There Is No Male or Female
Part of the Family
Put Your Hand in the Hand
The Servant Song
There Is a Quiet Understanding
We Are One in the Bond of Love
We Are One in the Spirit
We Gather Together to Ask the Lord's Blessing

Secular Songs

Black and White
Everything Is Beautiful
Living Together, Growing Together
The More We Get Together
Sing Hosea
Under One Sky (Ruth Pelham)
We Shall Overcome

Story

The story behind the writing of "Blest Be the Tie That Binds" (Osbeck, 1982, pp. 45-46)

Quotations

1. Revelations 7:9-12
2. There is neither Jew nor Greek, there is neither bond nor free, there is neither male nor female: for ye are all one in Christ Jesus.

Galatians 3:28 (KJV)

Discussion

1. How many brothers and sisters do you have?
2. When was the last time you were all together as a family? (For someone who's been married) How long have you and _____ been together/were you together?
3. Reminisce about groups or organizations they may have belonged to, including a certain church, the Legion, Elks, Masons, Ladies Auxiliary, etc.
4. Discuss their sense of unity with God.
5. Were you ever part of a very large choir? What kind of music did you sing?
6. Were you ever part of a large crowd that was cheering—for instance, when the King or Queen came to Canada? When the President was elected? When the end of World War II was declared?

Sensory Cue

You may want to join hands in unity when singing. You can also use a long, colorful ribbon or scarfs tied together for the group to hold onto to form a circle, especially when reaching out to each other is difficult, due to wheelchairs and physical limitations. Be wary that ribbon and materials such as this may be a distraction for the very confused.

Prayer

We are glad to be together today. Thank You for the people in this group. God, our Provider, You have made us so that we live in families. Help us when it gets difficult to be together and to live together. Soften our hearts by Your love. Thank You for Your forgiveness. Thank You for sticking with us. Thank You that Jesus prays for us all to be one. We pray in His Name. Amen.

H. McIlveen

Life Review

AGING

Hymns

Beyond the Sunset
From Days of Early Youth, O God
In Thee, O Lord, I Put My Trust
May Love Surround You
The Old Rugged Cross
Precious Lord, Take My Hand
Soon and Very Soon
Whatsoever You Do to the Least of My Brothers (verse 5)
Your Hands O Lord in Days of Old

Secular Songs

If I Had My Way
The Land Where We'll Never Grow Old
Old Folks at Home
Old Grey Mare
Silver Threads Among the Gold (especially verse 2)
Sunrise, Sunset (from *Fiddler on the Roof*)
When I Grow Too Old to Dream
When I'm Sixty-Four
When Your Hair Has Turned to Silver
Will You Love Me When I'm Old?
Young at Heart

Stories

1. Story of Caleb as a spy outside the Promised Land—Numbers
   13:26–14:9

2. Story of Caleb as a fighter entering the Promised Land—Joshua
    14:6–14

Quotation

Do not cast me off in the time of old age; do not forsake me when
my strength fails.

Psalm 71:9 (NKJV)

Discussion

1. What's it like to be old?
2. Are you old? Do you feel old?
3. What's it like to grow old?
4. Is getting older like wine and cheese—you get better with age?
5. Can you think of one advantage of getting old? A disadvantage?
6. What are you most afraid of when growing old?
7. Are you ever too old to dream? (Use with the song "When I
    Grow Too Old to Dream.")

Sensory Cue

Bring in some leaves, according to what season you're currently
in. Ask what each person's favorite season is and why. Pass the
leaves around the group for them to examine. Discuss old age as the
autumn of our lives.

Prayers

1. "The Elderly," from *The Hodder Book of Christian Prayers*
    #767–775 (Castle, 1986, pp. 215-219).

2. Be with me Lord, when I am old
    with silver threads among the gold;
    when summer's warm and winter's cold
    please take me in Your arms to hold,
    just like a sheep within the fold,
    Your love eternal I'll behold.
    Be with me Lord, when I am old.

K. Kirkland

Notes

1. Those with dementia often live in the past, and many believe they're much younger than they really are and need to be allowed to live in their own reality.
2. Use the second verse of "Silver Threads Among the Gold" to reinforce that they are loved for who they are, despite "faded cheeks or steps grown slow."

BIRTH

Hymns

Go, Tell It on the Mountain
Hark! The Herald Angels Sing
I Cannot Tell
I Wonder as I Wander
Long Ago, Prophets Knew
Mary's Little Boy Child
Night of Nights
O Holy Night
O Little Town of Bethlehem
O Sing a Song of Bethlehem
Tell Me the Story of Jesus
To a Virgin Meek and Mild

Secular Songs

Baby Face
Baby Shoes
Born Free
Hush Little Baby
Pretty Baby
Rock-a-Bye Baby
You Must Have Been a Beautiful Baby

Story

The Christmas Story—Luke 2:4-20

Discussion

1. (If you worked on a farm) Did you ever assist/help when lambs, calves, or colts were being born?
2. Did your dog ever have pups or your cat have kittens? Tell us what it was like. How did you feel—Excited? Happy? Disgusted? Sick to your stomach?

3. (If you had or have children) Were your children born at home?
4. What is childbirth like? (Women may have more expertise here!)
5. When you're just about to have a baby, what would it be like to travel or to be far away from home (like Mary on her way to Bethlehem)?

Sensory Cues

1. Show photos of babies clipped from magazines and mounted on cardboard backing.
2. Use a doll or furry stuffed animals (for example, a cat) to evoke responses and associations.
3. If someone on staff has recently had a baby, try to arrange a visit by the mother or father and baby.

Prayer

O God, creator of us all, we give You thanks for the life of this child. Grant us understanding, compassionate and affectionate hearts, and the gifts of courage and patience to face the challenge of caring for her/him; let Your love for us show forth in our lives, that we may create an atmosphere in which she/he will live a life full of dignity and worth. We ask this in the name of Jesus Christ our Lord, Amen.

H. McIlveen

CELEBRATION

Hymns

Christ the Lord Is Risen Today
He's Got the Whole World in His Hands
I Have the Joy, Joy, Joy
I'm Going to Sing When the Spirit Says Sing
Put Your Hand in the Hand
Rejoice and Be Glad
Rejoice, the Lord Is King
Whosoever Will

Secular Songs

Anniversary Waltz
Auld Lang Syne
Happy Birthday to You
Happy Days Are Here Again
Hava Nagilah
Wasn't That a Party?

Story

The celebration after the Exodus, in which Israel was delivered from slavery in Egypt—Exodus 15

Discussion

1. What kind of celebrations have you taken part in? Birthday parties? Anniversaries (perhaps their own wedding anniversary)? Graduations?
2. When World War II ended did you celebrate? How?
3. What would you celebrate today?
4. You might remind them that even seemingly little events can be celebrated, such as a sunrise, being together, feeling loved by God and those around you. Think of things that are cause for celebration every day.

Sensory Cues

1. Start the group with a balloon and bat it back and forth at one another—a good way to increase attention, alertness, and awareness of the theme.
2. Supply percussion instruments for the group to play along with the hymns.

Prayer

Thank you, Lord Jesus, for all our happiness. Thank you especially for the happiness that takes us by surprise. Above all we ask you to lead us toward the surprising discovery that what most pleases you will bring the greatest joy to us.

Jimmy Wallace
The Hodder Book of Christian Prayers
(Castle, 1986, p. 254)

CHANGE

Hymns

Abide with Me (verse 1)
All My Hope on God Is Founded
Be Still, My Soul
Glorious Things of Thee Are Spoken
Great Is Thy Faithfulness
His Eye Is on the Sparrow
Just as I Am, Without One Plea
The Servant Song
Through All the Changing Scenes of Life
Unto the Hills Around

Secular Songs

Cool Change (Little River Band)
Just the Way You Are (Billy Joel)
(There'll Be Bluebirds Over) the White Cliffs of Dover
There'll Be Some Changes Made
Tomorrow (from *Annie*)
Turn, Turn, Turn

Stories

1. The story of Job's losses (chapters 1 and 2) and later gains (chapter 42)
2. Selected verses from Psalm 90
3. Isaiah 61:1-7
4. The story of Rip Van Winkle
5. The story behind "I Need Thee Every Hour" (Osbeck, 1985, pp. 132-133).

Discussion

1. How have you changed through life?
2. Are you different than you were five years ago? If so, how?

3. Is change good or bad? Is it stressful?
4. How do you deal with change?
5. Give group members specific feedback on how you've seen them change through your time together.
6. How can we facilitate change? How does God create change?

Sensory Cue

Show old photos of the residents/staff; see if the group can recognize an earlier or contemporary photo of someone.

Prayer

God, give us grace to accept with serenity the things that cannot be changed, courage to change the things which should be changed, and the wisdom to distinguish the one from the other.

Reinhold Niebuhr
The Oxford Book of Prayer, p. 96

CHILDREN

Hymns

All God's Children Got Shoes
Away in a Manger
Can a Little Child Like Me?
Children, Go Where I Send Thee (black spiritual)
Children of Jerusalem
Children of the Heavenly Father
Come Children, Join to Sing
Dare to Be a Daniel
God Sees the Little Sparrow Fall (He Loves Me Too)
I Am So Glad That Our Father in Heaven
Jesus Loves Me
Jesus Loves the Little Children (Rebecca St. James)
Sometimes I Feel Like a Motherless Child
Tell Me the Story of Jesus
What Child Is This
When Mothers of Salem
The Wise May Bring Their Learning

Secular Songs

Children (from the TV series *Children of the World*)
The Greatest Love of All (Whitney Houston)
Teach Your Children Well

Story

Little children being brought to Jesus—Matthew 19:13-15 or Mark 10:13-16

Discussion

1. What do you enjoy most about children?
2. What do you find most cute?
3. What don't you like about children?

4. Did you ever dedicate your children to God—or have them baptized?
5. Why, do you think, Jesus wanted children to come to Him?
6. Would you like to be a child again? Why or why not?

Sensory Cues

1. Obtain pictures of the group's children. If unavailable, use magazine pictures that have been nonglare laminated.
2. If possible, have a small child come and be a part of the group.

Prayers

1. Now I lay me down to sleep,
   I pray the Lord my soul to keep
   If I should die before I wake,
   I pray the Lord my soul to take.

   Traditional Children's Prayer

2. From Witches, Warlocks, and Wurricoes,
   From Ghoulies, Ghosties, and Long-Leggit Beasties,
   From all Things that go bump in the night—
   Good Lord, deliver us!

   Traditional Cornish Prayer
   The Hodder Book of Christian Prayers
   (Castle, 1986, p. 129)

DEATH/LOSS

Hymns

Abide with Me
Amazing Grace
Be with Me
Christ Arose
Christ the Lord Is Risen Today
Deep River
Does Jesus Care? (verse 4)
Give Me Jesus (old spiritual)
Goin' Home
Great Is Thy Faithfulness
The Lord's My Shepherd
Nearer, My God, to Thee
Now Fades All Earthly Splendor
On Jordan's Stormy Banks I Stand
Rock of Ages, Cleft for Me
Soon and Very Soon
Tell It to Jesus
There'll Be Peace in the Valley
Will Your Anchor Hold (We Have an Anchor) (verse 3)

Secular Songs

Autumn Leaves
I Have a Dream
Massa's in the Cold, Cold Ground
Memories
Old Black Joe
Seasons in the Sun
Tears in Heaven (Eric Clapton)
Turn, Turn, Turn
When I Lost You

Story

John 11:17-37

Discussion

1. Do you remember the death of someone close to you? Who was it? How did you take it? Do you recall the circumstances? What happened? Were you able to grieve when you needed to?
2. Sometimes death is like winter, with spring around the corner. Talk about the cycle of the seasons as similar to the cycle of life.

Sensory Cue

Bring a picture or statue of "La Pieta," Mary holding the body of Jesus. Elicit thoughts, feelings, and associations as the statue is passed around the group.

Prayer

Lord Christ, shine upon all who are in the darkness of suffering or grief, that in your light they may receive hope and courage, and in your presence may find their rest and peace, for your love's sake.

Alan Warren
The Hodder Book of Christian Prayers
(Castle, 1986, p. 236)

DREAMS AND ASPIRATIONS

Hymns

All That I Am (verse 2)
Count Your Blessings
It Is More Than a Dream
Nearer, My God, to Thee (refers to Jacob's dream
    at Bethel—Genesis 28:10-22)
Where Dreams Come True (O. J. Smith/B. D. Ackley)
Whispering Hope

Secular Songs

All I Have to Do Is Dream
Bridge Over Troubled Water
Dream
Dream a Little Dream of Me
A Dream Is a Wish Your Heart Makes
Dream Your Troubles Away
I Got a Name (verse 3)
I Have a Dream (Abba)
The Impossible Dream
Last Night I Had the Strangest Dream (Pete Seeger)
Meet Me Tonight in Dreamland
There's a Long, Long Trail
When I Grow Too Old to Dream
When You Wish Upon a Star

Stories

1. Relate the contemporary story of a modern-day hero/heroine
    appropriate to the area you live in. Martin Luther King's "I
    have a dream" speech and vision may be appropriate.
2. The stories of Terry Fox, who ran across Canada to raise funds
    for cancer research then succumbed to it before completing his
    journey, and Amelia Earhart, who attempted a solo flight
    around the world, would also be suitable.

Quotations

1. In dreams begins responsibility.

   William Butler Yeats

2. You see things; and you say, "Why?" But I dream things that never were; and I say, "Why not?"

   George Bernard Shaw, 1921

3. You can also read Martin Luther King's speech, given at the Civil Rights March in Washington, DC, August 28, 1963, on "I have a dream."

Discussion

1. What dreams and hopes have you had in life?
2. Have you ever had a dream come true? If so, what?
3. Use career-related cues: Did you always want to be a _____?
4. Is there something you always wanted to do but didn't?
5. Do you have hopes for your children?
6. Have you ever persevered and worked hard to achieve something?

Sensory Cue

Bring in a Native American "dream catcher" to pass around the group, and explain the legend of how the spiderweb-like item functions.

Prayer

The words of any number of Evening Hymns would do nicely, for example:

> All praise to Thee my God this night
> when in the night I sleepless lie,
> my soul with heavenly thoughts supply;
> let no ill dreams disturb my rest,
> no powers of darkness me molest.

FRIENDSHIP

Hymns

Abide with Me
Hey Jesus, You're My Best Friend
I Heard the Voice of Jesus Say
In the Garden
I've Found a Friend, O Such a Friend
Jesus, Teacher and Friend
Leaning on the Everlasting Arms
My Sweet Lord
No, Not One!
O Jesus, Friend Unfailing
Our Great Savior
Tell It to Jesus
What a Friend We Have in Jesus
You'll Never Walk Alone (spiritual)

Secular Songs

Bridge Over Troubled Water
Diamonds Are a Girl's Best Friend
Good Friends?
Long Time Friends (Cathy Winter)
Song for Judith (Judy Collins)
Stand By Me
That's What Friends Are For
When You Come to the End of a Perfect Day
With a Little Help from My Friends (The Beatles)
You've Got a Friend (Carole King)

Stories

1. The story of David and Jonathan—I Samuel 18:1-15, 19:1-7, 20:1-42
2. The story of Jesus and the family of Mary, Martha, and Lazarus—Luke 10:38-42, John 11:1-44

Discussion

1. There's an old saying that goes, "A friend in need is a friend indeed." What does that mean? A true friend is one who stands by you and helps you when you need it.
2. Do you have a best friend? Who is/was your best friend?
3. Did you have many friends growing up? What makes a good friend? What did you share with your friend(s)?
4. Am I your friend? What do friends do together?
5. If Jesus were here now, would you want Him as a friend? Would He want you as a friend? (See John 15:12-15.)
6. What makes Jesus a good friend (you can tell him anything, he loves unconditionally, he always understands, forgives, etc.)? You can use this question with the hymn, "What a Friend We Have in Jesus."
7. Discuss this phrase: "A man that has friends must show himself friendly, and there is a friend that stays closer than a brother."—Proverbs 18:24
8. Can I be your friend?
9. Who's the best friend you've ever had?

Sensory Cue

Use pictures of the residents involved in social functions and activities.

Prayer

Good Lord Jesus, make me thankful for all you have given me in my friend. Bless him exceedingly above all that I can ask or think. Help us to be one in heart through all separations, to walk together in the path of Your service, and finally unite us in the place where love is perfect and immortal.

William Bright
The Hodder Book of Christian Prayers
(Castle, 1986, p. 221)

GOOD NEWS/BAD NEWS

Hymns

Good News

Alleluia, Give Thanks
From Ocean Unto Ocean
Go, Tell It on the Mountain
Good Christian Men, Rejoice and Sing
Good News (Chariot's A-Comin')
The Heavens Declare Thy Glory, Lord
Song of Good News
Surely Goodness and Mercy
We Love the Place, O God

Bad News

Nobody Knows the Trouble I've Seen

Secular Songs

Event-specific songs, such as war tunes, can be used here.

Get Happy
Hard Times (Stephen Foster)
Kum By Yah
Over There
We're in the Money (the end of the Depression)

Story

Reports of a revolt put down but also the death of the King's son—2 Samuel 18:19-33

Discussion

1. When's the last time you heard good news? What was it?
2. What's the best news you've ever heard? What's the worst news you've ever heard?

3. How can we soften bad news? Should we? Have you ever been told bad news? What was it?
4. How does good news make us feel? How does bad news make us feel?
5. How do we feel when we can tell someone good news? How do we feel when we have to tell someone bad news?
6. What good news does God tell us?

Sensory Cues

1. Bring in a newspaper and review some of the headlines at the start of the group.
2. Bring in a collection/reproductions of famous headlines, both good and bad, from newspapers.

Prayer

> Lord, you have sent me joy! I leap . . . I skip . . . it is good to be alive. You give life; you give the spirit of gladness to feel it. I love you. My sins are forgiven. It is good to be alive . . . and You have made it so.

Hubert van Zeller
The Hodder Book of Christian Prayers
(Castle, 1986, p. 253)

HOME

Hymns

Amazing Grace
Bless This House
Coming Home (Lord, I'm)
Goin' Home
Heaven Is My Home
Lead Me Gently Home, Father
Lead Me Home
The Old Home
The Prodigal Son
Softly and Tenderly Jesus Is Calling
Sometimes I Feel Like a Motherless Child
Swing Low, Sweet Chariot
This World Is Not My Home
Tryin' to Get Home (old spiritual)
Unless the Lord the House Shall Build
We Gather on Thy House
Whatsoever You Do to the Least of My Brothers
Would You Bless Our Homes and Families

Secular Songs

Back Home Again (John Denver)
Back Home Again in Indiana
Bill Bailey, Won't You Please Come Home?
Consider Yourself at Home
From His Canadian Home/Un Canadien Errant
Home (When Shadows Fall)
Home on the Range
Home Sweet Home
I'll Take You Home Again, Kathleen
Keep the Home Fires Burning
My Old Kentucky Home
Rolling Home
Take Me Home, Country Roads
When Johnny Comes Marching Home

Story

Jesus' promise to prepare a place for us: "In my Father's house are many mansions: if it were not so, I would have told you. I go to prepare a place for you. And if I go and prepare a place for you, I will come again, and receive you unto myself; that where I am, there you may be also."—John 14:1-4 (KJV)

Discussion

1. What's your home like? Who would be there?
2. Is heaven like home?
3. They say there's no place like home ("Home Sweet Home")— what does home mean to you?
4. Do you feel at home now? Does living here feel like home?
5. In the song "Softly and Tenderly Jesus Is Calling," what does it mean to "come home"?
6. Jesus said, "I go to prepare a place for you." What kind of home would you like prepared for you? Are you prepared to go to heaven?

Sensory Cue

Bring in pictures of houses, perhaps even actual photos of homes in which the group members lived.

Prayer

Dear God, homes mean a great deal to us: the home we were born in, the home we grew up and later spent our years in, the home we are in now, and the home You have prepared for us—our heavenly home where You welcome us. We pray that our special meaning of home will be alive in our hearts and souls. Amen.

H. McIlveen

LIFE'S STORMS AND TRIALS

Hymns

All My Trials
Amazing Grace
Count Your Blessings
From Every Stormy Wind That Blows
Heaven Is My Home (verse 2)
His Face in the Storm
I'll Stand By Until Morning
In the Hour of Trial
It Is Well with My Soul
Jesus Is Always There
Jesus, Lover of My Soul
Lift Me Gentle, Lord (Deborah Haines)
Master the Tempest Is Raging
My Anchor Holds
No, Not One!
O God, Our Help in Ages Past (verse 1)
On Jordan's Stormy Banks I Stand
A Shelter in the Time of Storm
Stand By Me (a gospel song by Charles Tondley)
Through All the Changing Scenes of Life
Whispering Hope
Why Should Cross and Trial Grieve Me?
Will Your Anchor Hold? (We Have An Anchor)

Secular Songs

Bridge Over Troubled Water
Hard Times Come Again No More
Look for the Silver Lining
The Morning After
Singin' in the Rain
Stand By Me
Stormy Weather
You'll Never Walk Alone

Story

Jesus and a storm—Mark 4:35-41

Poem

God gives to His servants a promise:
You'll not have to face life alone,
For when you grow weak in your struggle,
His strength will prevail—not your own.

Hess

(Source: "Our Daily Bread: Working in God's Garden, "July 1, 1998. Online. July 12, 1998. Grand Rapids, MI: RBC Ministries. Available: *http://www.gospelcom.net/rbc/odb/odb-07-01-98.html*)

Discussion

1. Do you like thunderstorms?
2. What do you do when you see lightning and hear thunder?
3. What's it like to be in a snowstorm?
4. Do you know what a hurricane/tornado/twister is? Have you ever seen one?
5. Have you weathered a storm in your life?
6. Some people have stormy marriages or relationships—do you know anyone like that?
7. How do you handle the stormy times in your life?
8. When you look back on your life, would you say it was calm or stormy? Why?

Sensory Cues

1. Light a candle to create a slightly darkened room.
2. Use the story behind "Amazing Grace" (Osbeck, 1982, p. 16).
3. Use the story behind "Blessed Assurance," written by blind poet Fanny Crosby, who wrote some 8,000 hymns, despite her blindness (Osbeck, 1982, p. 42).

Prayer

> Jesus, Deliverer!
> Come thou to me:
> Sooth thou my voyaging
> Over Life's sea.
> Thou, when the storm of Death
> Roars, sweeping by,
> Whisper, O Truth of Truth—
> "Peace! It is I."

Anatolius (Fifth century)
The Hodder Book of Christian Prayers
(Castle, 1986, p. 238)

NAME

Hymns

All Hail the Power of Jesus' Name
At the Name of Jesus
Hallelujah, Praise Jehovah
How Sweet the Name of Jesus Sounds
Lord, Our Lord, Thy Glorious Name
"Man of Sorrows," What a Name
O Lord, Our Lord in All the Earth
O Praise Ye the Name of Jehovah
Our Father, Clothed with Majesty
When All Thy Names Are One

Secular Songs

There are numerous songs with people's first names in the titles, too many to list here in their entirety—some may be in your group.

Alice Blue Gown
Billy Boy
Clementine
Goodnight Irene
I Got a Name
If You're Irish, Come into the Parlor
I'll Take You Home Again, Kathleen
I'm Just Wild About Harry
Jean
Juanita
Louise
MacNamara's Band
Maria (from *West Side Story*)
Mary's a Grand Old Name
Molly Malone
Once in Love with Amy
Oh, Donna
Peg O' My Heart

Ramona
Sioux City Sue
Sweet Adeline
Sweet Lorraine
You've Got a Friend

Stories

1. God speaking to the boy Samuel—I Samuel 3:1-20
2. Discuss the origins of the name of the city, town, and/or state or province you live in. For example, Vancouver, BC and Vancouver, Washington were named after Britain's Captain George Vancouver who was seeking the Northwest Passage in 1792 in his ship, the *Discovery.*

   (Sources: *http://www.book.uci.edu/Books/Moon/vancouver.html;* Conn, Heather, "Early Coastal Explorers," in Davis, Chuck, ed. *The Greater Vancouver Book.* Vancouver, BC: The Linkman Press. Online. July 1/98. Available: *http://www.discovervancouver.com/ vancouverbook/earlyex3.htm*)

Quotation

His name will be called Wonderful Counselor, Mighty God, Everlasting Father, Prince of Peace.

Isaiah 9:6 (NJKV)

Discussion

1. What is your first name? Last name?
2. What was your name before you got married? (This can be really difficult for some to remember. Sometimes you can access this information by asking them their mother's first name, their father's first name, then "What was your father's name: John _____;" they will sometimes fill in the blank).
3. How did you get your name—were you named after someone? An aunt or relative? The names we give our children often refer to the hopes we have for them. Do you have children? What are their names?

Sensory Cues

1. Bring along a book of names and their meanings. Read out what each person's name means.
2. Write out what each person's name means in large-print type, and have each read it if possible, or have one group member read them all. At every opportunity, let them do for themselves.

Prayer

> Thank You for the familiar sound of my name. Thank You that it has always been with me and always will stay with me. Thank You that You know my name—even though others may forget—and that You call me by my name. We pray in the name of the one who was named Jesus, "Savior." Amen.

H. McIlveen

Note

Secular songs with personal names in them abound. Remember that not everyone wants to hear that same old familiar song with their name in it. On occasion, I've met people who were tired of hearing the song associated with their name, such as Irene for "Goodnight, Irene" or Alice for "Alice Blue Gown."

SAYING GOOD-BYE

Hymns

Abide with Me
Be Still, My Soul
Blest Be the Tie That Binds
Give Me Jesus
God Be with You Till We Meet Again
God Will Take Care of You
How Firm a Foundation
May the Good Lord Bless and Keep You Till We Meet Again
Nearer My God to Thee
O Love That Will Not Let Me Go
Sing a New Song to the Lord
Softly and Tenderly Jesus Is Calling

Secular Songs

Aloha Oe
Auld Lang Syne
Fare Thee Well (The Rankin Family)
Goodbye, Good Luck, God Bless You
Goodnight, It's Time to Go
I'll Be Seeing You
Let the Rest of the World Go By
May Love Surround You
Now Is the Hour
Seasons in the Sun
Smile the While (Till We Meet Again)
Turn, Turn, Turn
We'll Meet Again
When Day Is Done
Wish Me Luck as You Wave Me Good-Bye

Stories

1. Jesus saying good-bye to his close friends—John 13:33, 14:4
2. Jacob's blessing of his children and his death—Genesis 49-50:7
3. The hymn stories associated with departure: "Abide with Me" and "Blest Be the Tie That Binds" (Osbeck, 1982, p. 45)

Discussion

1. Do you like saying good-bye?
2. Have you had to say many good-byes in your life?
3. What has helped you with difficult good-byes?
4. What was the most difficult good-bye? Why?
5. What eases the pain of a good-bye?
6. Are men less likely to cry than women?
7. Is there someone you knew that you never got the chance to say good-bye to? Who would that be?
8. If he or she were here right now, what would you say? Imagine that this person is here right now—what would you like to say to him/her?
9. Have you ever said good-bye and left with hard feelings?

Sensory Cues

1. Bring in old photographs of family members.
2. Compile scrapbooks of memorabilia of the group.

Prayer

> Almighty God, Father of all mercies and giver of all comfort: Deal graciously, we pray, with those who mourn, that casting every care on You, they may know the consolations of Your love, through Jesus Christ our Lord.
>
> *Book of Common Prayer, Oxford, p. 249*

Note

This theme is useful when a group member has died or is moving/leaving. If the group (or staff) member who is leaving is at the group, encourage members one by one to offer their farewell to experience proper closure. You might say something such as, "Doris is leaving tomorrow to live somewhere else. Is there anything you'd like to say to her before she goes?"

SIBLINGS

Hymns

Childhood songs, such as:

God Sees the Little Sparrow Fall (He Loves Me Too)
He's Got the Whole World in His Hands
Jesus Loves Me
Jesus Loves the Little Children
The Servant Song
Sisters and Brothers
Thank You (verse 2)

Secular Songs

Brother, Can You Spare a Dime?
Consider Yourself At Home
He Ain't Heavy, He's My Brother
Let There be Peace on Earth
We Are Family

Stories

1. Jacob and Esau—Genesis 27
2. Joseph and his brothers—Genesis 37-46

Discussion

1. Did you have brothers or sisters? Do you remember their names? Was there one you were particularly close to?
2. Were you the oldest, youngest, or in the middle? An only child?
3. Did you compete with your siblings? For parents' attention? For excellence in school?
4. How would/did it make you feel if a father/mother favored one of your brothers/sisters?
5. Did you have quarrels with your siblings? Did you have to keep peace between two of your siblings?

Sensory Cues

1. Obtain old photographs, where possible, of the siblings of those in the group.
2. Bring in other photos of family scenes—parents with newborns or large families.

Prayer

Generous God, You have placed us in families so that we would not be lonely. Thank You for brothers or sisters—for happy memories of them—for companionship with them—for their accomplishments that made us proud. Where we've had a falling out with them, forgive us. Help us to be healed of hurts inflicted on us in our family. Make us one, even as You are one. For Your love's sake. Amen.

H. McIlveen

SPOUSES/PARTNERS

Hymns

The Greatest Thing in All the World
I Will Celebrate Your Love Forever, Yahweh (Psalm 89)
Love Divine, All Loves Excelling
O Perfect Love, All Human Thought Transcending
The Servant Song
This Is My Commandment

Secular Songs

There are many well-known songs from bygone eras that are about relationships. You might know of particular favorites among the group. Some suggestions here include:

Always
Down by the Old Mill Stream
Forever and Ever
Get Me to the Church on Time (from *My Fair Lady*)
It Had to Be You
Let Me Call You Sweetheart
Love and Marriage
Make Believe
Sometime
You Were Meant for Me

Stories

1. The romance/choosing of Ruth and Boaz (see the Book of Ruth)
2. Contemporary stories of happy unions or a unique circumstance surrounding how two people met (Ann Landers is a good source for these stories.)

Discussion

1. Tell us about _____. What was/is he/she like? Do you remember how you met? What did she/he do for a living? What did/do

you like about him/her? How did she/he make you feel? Do you think of him/her often? Do you miss him/her? What kind of things did you do together? What one quality did you like best about her/him (kind, good sense of humor, handsome, pretty, etc.)?
2. Who is the love of your life? Were you attracted to each other right away?

Sensory Cues

1. Use photos or memorabilia/reminders of their companions.
2. If you don't already know, find out the names of their companions.

Prayer

> O Lord, we pray for those who full of confidence and love, once chose a partner for life, and are now alone. May hurt and bitterness and sadness be redeemed by healing and love, personal weakness by your strength, inner despair by the joy of knowing you and serving others, through Jesus Christ our Lord.

H. McIlveen

Note

Remember that not everyone had a good relationship. Some may be divorced, some may have never married, and some may have had a marriage/relationship that they don't want to talk about because it's very private to them. It's important to respect how much they're willing to self-disclose, without coming across as prying.

TEACHER

Hymns

Let Children Hear the Mighty Deeds
Lord, I Lift My Soul to Thee
Lord, to Me Thy Ways Make Known
My People, Give Ear, Attend to My Word
Savior, Teach Me, Day by Day
Teach Me the Measure of My Days
Thy Word Sheds Light Upon My Path
Unto Thee, O Lord Jehovah
When Morning Lights the Eastern Skies

Secular Songs

Que Sera Sera (verse 2)
School Days
Teach Me Tonight
Teach Your Children Well

Stories

1. Ann Sullivan who rescued/shaped Helen Keller's life and was known as "Teacher"
2. Greek mythology—*Mentor* the teacher, role model, encourager, shaper, confidante of Telemachus, the son of King Odysseus of Ithaca (See Hamilton, 1942, pp. 296-297.)
3. Jesus teaching—Luke 12

Poem

The Tutor

A tutor who tooted the flute
Tried to teach two young tooters to toot.
Said the two to the tutor,
"Is it harder to toot, or
To tutor two tooters to toot?"

Carolyn Wells
(Hamlyn, 1932, p. 11)

Discussion

1. Did anyone here ever teach school?
2. Do you know someone in your family who is a teacher?
3. Remember the expression "teacher's pet"? Were you ever the teacher's pet? Can you recall having a favorite teacher in school? What was she/he like?
4. What town were you born in? (Have this information with you in case they can't remember.) Did you go to school there? Do you remember a teacher you had when you were in school? What was her/his name? Was she/he strict? What did you like about her/him?
5. At the start of a school day, did the class pray? Sing? ("O Canada!"? "The Star Spangled Banner"? "The Maple Leaf Forever"? "My Country 'Tis of Thee?" Others?)
6. Who has been a teacher or major influence in your life? Who is someone you respect, someone who made a difference in who you are?
7. What do we learn from God? What does Jesus teach us about how to live?

Sensory Cues

1. An apple—for the teacher
2. Pictures of old schoolhouses

Prayer

We honor You, O God, and we honor those who have been our teachers. Thank You for the skills and subjects they taught. But thank You, too, for the way they influenced the way we live. For ways in which we have taught others, also, we give thanks. Even though we may have forgotten their names, we are grateful that You, Our God, have not forgotten our work. In the Name of the Teacher who spoke words of eternal life, even Jesus. Amen.

H. McIlveen

TRANSITIONS/MOVES

Hymns

Abide with Me
All the Way My Savior Leads Me
Guide Me, O Thou Great Jehovah
Hark, Hark My Soul (pilgrimage song)
He Leadeth Me, O Blessed Thought
He's Got the Whole World in His Hands
I Know Not Where the Road Will Lead
Jesus, Savior, Pilot Me
O God, Our Help in Ages Past
A Pilgrim Was I and A-Wand'ring
Precious Lord, Take My Hand
Through All the Changing Scenes of Life
When My Last Hour Is Close at Hand

Secular Songs

By the Rivers of Babylon
Bye, Bye, Blackbird
Cool Change (Little River Band)
Gotta Move On
Happy Wanderer
Keep Right on to the End of the Road
Pack Up Your Troubles
So Long
There'll Be Some Changes Made
Turn, Turn, Turn
Where Have All the Flowers Gone?

Stories

1. Psalm 137:1-6
2. Ruth 1:16-17
3. The story of Edward Hopper, who wrote the hymn "Jesus, Savior, Pilot Me." He ministered to a seaside congregation, many of whom were seamen, and died sitting in his armchair

with a half-finished poem about heaven on his lap (Osbeck, 1985, pp. 163-165)

Discussion

1. Where were you born?
2. What was it like the first time you left home—was that when you got married?
3. What's it like to be homesick—how does it feel?
4. Do you get homesick at Christmas?
5. Did you ever move to a place that you didn't like?
6. What helps you feel better after a move—a familiar object? A trip back to your former house? Seeing a familiar friend? Making a new friend? Singing an old familiar song? Pictures, mementos?
7. What will it be like when we "move to heaven"?
8. What have you had to leave behind (family, home)?
9. Why did you come to live here? What brought you to _____?
10. Was the move stressful?
11. Have you always lived in the same place? Moved often?
12. What was it like to come to live here at _____?
13. How do you deal with changes? Would you say you're easygoing? High-strung?

Sensory Cues

1. Show a picture of a bridge or hold a discussion about a local bridge.
2. Talk about the passenger ships that brought many citizens to the new country (perhaps they were on such a ship).
3. Bring a suitcase to the group meeting. Individuals may recognize it and be able to link it to moving/traveling.

Prayers

1. Read Psalm 139:7-10.
2. God, you are the same, yesterday, today, and forever. Whenever we move, you always go with us and get there ahead of us. Still our worries, we pray. Help us to know that we are in the palm of Your hand. Through Christ. Amen.

H. McIlveen

Note

Transition from home to a residential facility can be difficult and stressful for the elderly person. Stories about displaced people in the Bible can be a bridge to discussing feelings the residents may be going through concerning their transition.

WORK

Hymns

Bringing in the Sheaves
In Our Work and in Our Play
Joyful, Joyful, We Adore Thee
Lord of All Power, I Give You My Will
May the Mind of Christ My Savior
O Hasten, Let Me Walk with Thee
Revive Thy Work, O Lord
What a Friend We Have in Jesus
Work, for the Night Is Coming
A Workman in a Village Home
Your Work, O Lord, Needs Many Hands

Secular Songs

If I Were a Carpenter
I've Been Workin' on the Railroad
Nice Work if You Can Get It
9 to 5 (Dolly Parton)
Whistle While You Work

Stories

1. The Creation story, Genesis 1 and 2, especially references by God to his work as being "good"
2. Martha and Mary entertaining Jesus, one doing all the work and the other "shirking" her duty—Luke 10:38-42

Quotation

Come unto me, all ye that labour and are heavy laden, and I will give you rest. Take my yoke upon you, and learn of me; for I am meek and lowly in heart: and ye shall find rest unto your souls. For my yoke is easy, and my burden is light.

Matthew 11:28-30 (KJV)

Discussion

1. What kind of work did you do (do you do)?
2. Have you ever been out of work (for example, during the great Depression)?
3. Is it easy or difficult to find a job?
4. What task (in or outside the house) did you find most satisfying? (Patient/resident social histories will sometimes help when the individual can't remember.)
5. Did you like best to work alone or in the company of others?
6. How could you tell when you had done a good job?
7. Do you like to start a task or finish one?
8. Discuss the old saying, "A man works from sun to sun, a woman's work is never done."
9. Have you ever done volunteer work?
10. Did anyone here ever live on a farm? What kind of chores did you do?

Sensory Cues

1. Help the residents trace their hands on cardboard and then cut out the outlines. Reflect on what our hands have done throughout our lives.
2. Bring in some tools of various trades (for example, thimble and needle, hammer, typewriter).

Prayer

> May the favor of the Lord our God rest upon us; establish the work of our hands for us—yes, establish the work of our hands.
>
> *Psalm 90:17 (NIV)*

Sensory

ARMS

Hymns

Children of the Heavenly Father
Fight the Good Fight with All Thy Might (verse 4)
Here, O My Lord, I See Thee Face to Face (verse 5)
I Am So Glad That Our Father in Heaven (verse 2)
It Is No Secret What God Can Do
Lean on His Arms
Leaning on the Everlasting Arms
Once in Royal David's City (verse 3)
Safe in the Arms of Jesus
What a Friend We Have in Jesus

Secular Songs

Embraceable You
I Can Help
I Got Lost in His Arms
My Honey's Lovin' Arms
Put Your Arms Around Me, Honey

Story

Luke 15:11-32, especially verse 20—"threw his arms around him and kissed him"

Discussion

1. What do we do with our arms (e.g., lean, hug, hold, extend, reach)?

2. What would we miss if we couldn't use our arms? What do we miss because we can't use our arm/arms (e.g., because of a stroke)?
3. Do you remember what your mother's arms were like? Your father's?
4. When you were married, did you offer someone your arm or take someone's arm?
5. Who would you like to hug you?
6. Discuss the following phrases: arm in arm, arm's length, with open arms, within arm's reach, to bear arms, lay down one's arms, up in arms.

Sensory Cues

1. Demonstrate different arm movements, such as hailing a taxi, announcing you have a bingo, shaking a fist at someone, waving good-bye, imitating a chicken.
2. Do hand-in-hand swaying and movement to music.

Prayer

Dear Lord, today we give thanks for all the work and deeds our arms have done for us throughout the years. For holding, for hugging, for lifting and carrying, for touching and embracing. We take comfort that You hold us in Your everlasting arms. We feel the depth of Your love. For all your goodness, Lord, we are truly blessed. Amen.

K. Kirkland

CLOTHING

Hymns

All God's Children Got Shoes
Be Thou My Vision
Beyond! (verse 3)
The Christian's Good-Night (verse 5)
Dear Lord and Father of Mankind (verse 1)
Down by the Riverside
Fairest Lord Jesus (verse 2)
Golden Slippers
The Hem of His Garment
O Worship the King, All Glorious Above (verse 2)
Put on the Garment of Praise
This Is My Rest Forever

Secular Songs

Alice Blue Gown
Bell-Bottom Trousers
Buttons and Bows
Down by the Old Mill Stream ("dressed in gingham, too")
Easter Bonnet
Greensleeves
On the Sunny Side of the Street ("Get your coat and grab your hat")
Put on Your Old Gray Bonnet
Scarlet Ribbons
School Days ("You were my queen in calico")
She Wore a Yellow Ribbon
A Shine on Your Shoes
Who Threw the Overalls in Mrs. Murphy's Chowder?

Stories

1. The woman who touches the hem of Jesus' garment—Luke 8:40-48
2. Garment of praise—Isaiah 61
3. Psalm 132:9 (relates to the hymn "This Is My Rest Forever")

Discussion

1. Begin the group by drawing attention to what the members of the group are wearing.
2. Do you know how to sew? Discuss the use of different materials: cotton, wool, calico, gingham, etc.
3. Wrap a stole around one person and speak to the group about how God loves, cares for, and keeps them.
4. Use clothing that may be associated with memories, such as a military uniform, a cap, a wedding dress, a baby's bonnet. Ask them about their wedding or baby. "How did you feel the day you got married?"
5. Where did you get that beautiful dress?
6. Do you like to shop for clothes? Have you ever made your own clothes?
7. Did anyone ever get "hand-me-downs" when they were growing up?
8. Who is a man (or woman) of the "cloth"?
9. In the hymn "The Hem of His Garment," someone is healed by touching the clothes of Jesus. Imagine what it would be like to be touched and healed by Jesus. How would you feel? (Hands-on prayer may be appropriate here.)

Sensory Cues

1. Bring in some different clothing materials in an array of textures and colors—pass them around the group for them to feel and see. Don't hesitate to bring something glitzy that will catch their attention.
2. Pass around pictures of different clothing styles throughout the eras, including some of today's more outrageous fashions. Elicit memories, comments, and opinions.

Prayer

We thank You, O God, you who are a good provider, for the clothing we wear. Thank You for clothing that gives us a lift and for clothing that makes us feel secure. Thank You for clothing that we wear when we celebrate. Thank you also that You welcome us home, you hug us, put new clean clothes on us, and celebrate.

Just as You "clothe" the flowers with their beautiful colors, so You provide us with the clothing that we need. You also wrap us round with a sense of Your care. Thank You for both kinds of "clothing" and all other tokens of Your love. When we feel discouraged, may others help us to put on a garment of praise to replace the spirit of heaviness. This we pray through Christ. Amen.

H. McIlveen

DARKNESS

Hymns

Begin with the theme of darkness through hymns and move toward songs about light:

Abide with Me; Fast Falls the Eventide
Be Not Afraid
It Is No Secret What God Can Do
Jesus Bids Us Shine
Lead, Kindly Light
Love Lifted Me
Prayer of St. Francis (Make Me a Channel of Your Peace) (verse 2)
Morning Has Broken
Nobody Knows the Trouble I've Seen
The Servant Song
Shine, Jesus, Shine
Somebody Cares for Me
This Little Light of Mine
Turn Your Eyes upon Jesus
Whispering Hope

Secular Songs

April Showers
Dream Your Troubles Away
Let the Sun Shine In
Look for the Silver Lining
Look to the Rainbow
Somewhere Over the Rainbow
You Are My Sunshine
You'll Never Walk Alone

Stories

1. A number of biblical stories happen at night—usually there is the presence of fear, often relieved by an agent of "light."

2. Jesus, walking on the water—Mark 6:47-52
3. Paul and Silas in prison—Acts 16:16-31
4. The announcement to the shepherds—Luke 2:8-20
5. Robert Martin's *My Journey into Alzheimer's*

Discussion

1. What was the darkest moment in your life?
2. What was of help to you in that darkness?
3. What is the physically darkest situation you can remember (being in a cellar when the lights went out, being outdoors in the country on a starless night)? How did you feel in the dark?
4. When you were little, did you check under your bed at night?
5. Why does the dark frighten us?

Sensory Cue

Light a candle in the center of the circle.

Prayers

The Hodder Book of Christian Prayers (Castle, 1986):

1. page 18, #20—Saint Augustine
2. page 65, #196—Saint Augustine
3. page 113, #384—Jeremy Taylor
4. page 1378, #468—T. S. Eliot

Note

Reflect on the answer you, as group facilitator, would give to the question, "What was the darkest moment in your life?"

FACES

Hymns

Be Not Afraid
Come, Ye Disconsolate, Where'er Ye Languish
Face to Face with Christ My Savior
God and Man at Table Are Sat Down
Here, O My Lord, I See Thee Face to Face
His Blessed Face
His Eye Is on the Sparrow
I Heard the Voice of Jesus Say
O That Will Be Glory
We Have Come into His House

Secular Songs

Baby Face
Be a Clown
The First Time Ever I Saw Your Face
Funny Face
I See Your Face Before Me
Powder Your Face with Sunshine
Smiles
You Must Have Been a Beautiful Baby

Stories

1. God speaking to Moses face-to-face—Exodus 33:7-11
2. Moses' face shone—Exodus 34:29-35

Discussion

1. Make this an awareness exercise by discussing the different faces of the group. Have all members focus on each person, perhaps as you stand behind each in turn. "Look around the group—whose face do you recognize?"
2. Pass around a photo or two of a staff member or group member and ask if they recognize the face. Highlight positive features

and elicit comments about eye color, skin, hair, smile, ethnic background (does she look Irish?), glasses. Allow and encourage the residents to feel your face with their hands—noting whiskers, eyebrows, nose, lips, contours. Pass around a large picture of Jesus. Ask if they recognize who it is. "Does he look familiar? Is he someone you know?"

Sensory Cues

1. Talk about making faces. Demonstrate what you can communicate with your face: frown, smile, grimace (as in a bad taste), surprise, sadness.
2. Show pictures of different facial expressions.
3. Let them try a scented facial cream.

Prayer

The Lord bless you and keep you;
the Lord make His face shine upon you,
and be gracious to you;
the Lord lift up His countenance upon you,
and give you peace.

Numbers 6:24-26 (NKJV)

Note

Many people, especially family, are disappointed that cognitively impaired elderly can't remember their names, even in person. Rather than asking "What's my name?" or "Who am I?" keep it simpler. "Do I look familiar?" is much easier to answer and a better starting point. The memory for names is stored in the brain separately from the more meaningful data of what you know and feel about someone. The same can be done with music: "Does it sound familiar?" or "Is that a familiar song?"

GARDENING

Hymns

Fairest Lord Jesus
For the Beauty of the Earth
God Who Touches Earth with Beauty
God Sees the Little Sparrow Fall (He Loves Me Too) (verses 2,3)
In a Monastery Garden
In the Beautiful Garden of Prayer
In the Garden
Morning Has Broken (verse 2)
Thy World Is Like a Garden, Lord

Secular Songs

Amapola
April Showers (Al Jolson)
Bluebells of Scotland
Daisy, Daisy
Edelweiss
English Country Garden
Honeysuckle Rose
Jeannine, I Dream of Lilac Time
My Wild Irish Rose
O My Love Is Like a Red, Red Rose
Oats, Peas, Beans and Barley Grow
Paper Roses
Ramblin' Rose
Red Roses for a Blue Lady
The Rose (Bette Midler)
Rose of Tralee
Sweet Violets
Tiptoe Through the Tulips (Tiny Tim)
When You Wore a Tulip
The Yellow Rose of Texas

Stories

1. Jesus in the garden of Gethsemane—Mark 14: 32-42
2. The story of a young man who experienced something similar to the hymn "In the Garden" in the book *A Window to Heaven* by Diane Komp, pp. 42-44
3. The parable of the sower—Mark 4 or Luke 8

Quotation

- five rows of "peas"—prayer, preparedness, promptness, perseverance, politeness
- three rows of "squash"—squash gossip, criticism, and indifference
- five rows of "lettuce"—let us love one another, let us be faithful, let us be loyal, let us be unselfish, let us be truthful
- three rows of "turnips"—turn up for church, turn up with a new idea, turn up with the determination to do a better job than you did yesterday

Kemmons Wilson
founder of an International motel chain

(Source: "Our Daily Bread: Working on God's Garden," July 6, 1998. Online. July 12, 1998. Grand Rapids, MI: RBC Ministries. Available:*http://www.gospelcom.net/rbc/odb/odb-07-06-98.html*)

Discussion

1. Did you ever do any gardening?
2. Do/did you like to garden? Did you have a specialty?
3. Recite the old children's rhyme, "Mary, Mary, quite contrary, how does your garden grow? . . . "
4. What did you grow (favorite types of flowers and vegetables)?
5. Did you ever make preserves or do canning?
6. Have you ever heard the old expression, "Doesn't that jar your mother's preserves!"? What does it mean?
7. What is it about gardening that appeals to you?

8. Was your garden a quiet place? What garden smells or scents do you remember?

Sensory Cues

1. Bring in some fresh preserves that the group can smell and taste, such as raspberry jam. You might use this as a treat to start the group or for after it's over, along with a hot cup of tea or coffee. Another idea is to bring in fresh flowers that can be passed around, smelled, and named, You could also bring in a package of seeds or a bulb and plant it with the group in a pot that can be kept in your meeting area. Each week the group can be reminded of the plant the group is growing.
2. Tell the story behind the hymn "In the Garden" (Osbeck, 1982, p. 124).
3. Hold the group outdoors if possible.

Prayer

Lord, teach us to work with love, knowing that work is love made visible. To sow seeds with tenderness and reap the harvest with joy, even as if you were to eat the fruit. To change all things we fashion with a breath of our own spirit, and to know that all the blessed dead are standing about us and watching.

Kahlil Gibran
The Hodder Book of Christian Prayers
(Castle, 1986, pp. 300-301)

HAIR

Hymns

And She Washed It Away with Her Hair
The Head That Once Was Crowned with Thorns
I Heard the Voice of Jesus Say (verse 1)
Jesus, Lover of My Soul (verse 2)
The Lord My Shepherd Guards Me Well (verse 3)
The Lord's My Shepherd I'll Not Want (verse 4)
When I Survey the Wondrous Cross (verse 3)

Secular Songs

And Her Golden Hair Was Hanging Down Her Back
Black Is the Color of My True Love's Hair
Black Velvet Band
Jeannie with the Light Brown Hair
Scarlet Ribbons
Silver Threads Among the Gold
Sioux City Sue ("Your hair is red, your eyes are blue")
When Your Hair Has Turned to Silver
Why Don't You Love Me Like You Used to Do?

Story

The woman who wiped Jesus' feet with her hair—Luke 7:36-48

Discussion

1. Discuss how your hair changes color through the years (going grey; dyeing it).
2. Talk about different hairstyles—brush cut, Afro, perm, marcelled—and different looks, such as straight, wavy, curly, wooly, frizzy, peppercorn, salt and pepper, bald is beautiful.
3. Recount famous stories: *Rapunzel, The Three Little Pigs* ("Not by the hair of my chinny chin chin").
4. Discuss some hair expressions: hairline, hairdresser, hairdo, haircut, hairbreadth, won by a hair, hair shirt, hair-raiser, hair-

pin, hairpiece, let one's hair down, hair trigger, hairsplitter, he didn't turn a hair, against the hair, makes one's hair stand on end, made one want to pull one's hair out.

Sensory Cues

1. Draw their attention to the hairstyles of the different members of the group.
2. Look at pictures of different hairstyles, both old-fashioned and contemporary. Elicit opinions.

Prayer

Thank You, God our Provider, for those who care for our hair, helping us to feel better about ourselves. Thank You for Your care of us—so detailed that You know even the number of our hairs. For texture and color and style—signs of Your creativity and of our uniqueness, we give thanks. In the Name of Jesus, we pray. Amen.

H. McIlveen

HANDS/TOUCH

Hymns

At Even' Ere the Sun Was Set
God Who Touches Earth with Beauty
He Leadeth Me, O Blessed Thought
He Touched Me
Heal Me, Hands of Jesus
He's Got the Whole World in His Hands
Jesus' Hands Were Kind Hands
Lay Your Hands
Not What These Hands Have Done
Precious Lord, Take My Hand
Put Your Hand in the Hand
The Servant Song
Take My Life and Let It Be
The Touch of His Hand on Mine
Your Hand, O Lord

Secular Songs

Can't Help Falling in Love
Hands Across the Table
I Wanna Hold Your Hand
In the Good Old Summertime
Mexican Clap Hands Song (Chiapanecas)
Take These Hands (Patricia McKernon)

Stories

1. The conversion of Saul of Tarsus; blinded, he had to be led by the hand—Acts 9:1-9
2. The woman was healed when she reached out and touched Jesus—Luke 8:40-48
3. Jesus heals a blind man by laying his hands upon him—Mark 8:22-26
4. The woman with the hemorrhage touches Jesus—Mark 5:25-34
5. A deaf and mute man is healed—Mark 7:31-37

Quotation

And he took them up in His arms, put His hands upon them, and blessed them.

Mark 10:16 (KJV)

Discussion

1. Discuss the importance of hands. What do we do with our hands?
2. Discuss "hand" expressions: "I've got to hand it to you," "It was touch and go," "I've been out of touch," "Isn't he touchy?"
3. What kind of work have your hands done?
4. Do you express yourself through touch? Are you comfortable being hugged or giving hugs?
5. Do you like your hands (appearance)?
6. What can we tell about people by looking at or feeling their hands?
7. What can we communicate through our hands?
8. What can hands do (touch, hold, grab, exert pressure, point, push, pinch, caress, make a fist)?
9. What work or play have you done with your hands (play piano, knit, crochet, bake, sew, chop wood, milk cows, harness horses, paint, write letters)?
10. What do you wish you could still do with your hands?

Sensory Cues

1. Start the group by asking each person to shake hands with the person next to her/him.
2. Draw an outline of their hands.
3. Ask the group to identify the meaning of certain hand signals: pointing a finger, wagging a finger, making a fist, thumbs up/ down, victory sign ("V").
4. Offer them a tactile experience: give them some scented hand cream to try (if they'd like); you may need to assist with rub-

bing the cream into the skin of their hands. Ask them how it feels and smells.

5. Encourage the people to clap their hands together to the beat of the music.

6. Bring drums/percussion instruments along or ask the clients to clap to the music.

7. Pass an unfamiliar percussion or musical instrument around the group—see if they know how it works. Encourage them to explore its feel and sound. Convey that there's really no "wrong" way to play it—be open to creative ways of expression! You can also use items with unusual textures to encourage members to explore different tactile sensations.

Prayers

1. Where possible, participants are in a circle and can touch one another during prayer.

> Take my life and let it be
> consecrated, Lord, to thee;
> take my hands and let them move
> at the impulse of thy love;
>
> Take my feet, and let them be
> swift and beautiful for thee.
> Take my voice and let me sing
> always, only, for my King.
>
> *from the hymn* "Take My Life and Let It Be"
> *(Havergal/Malan)*

2. God, we give thanks for the people here, and the fact that we can touch each other. Thank you for all the things that we can touch, for people who have lovingly touched us. Thank you that you, God, touch us deep within us and that we are in the palm of your hand. In Jesus' name we pray, Amen.

> *H. McIlveen*

HEARING (EARS)

Hymns

Amazing Grace
Cause Me to Hear
Do You Hear What I Hear?
For the Beauty of the Earth (verse 3)
Hear Our Prayer, O Lord
Holy Spirit, Hear Us
I Heard the Voice of Jesus Say
In the Garden
Listen, Listen, Listen
Lord, I Was Blind
O for a Thousand Tongues to Sing (verse 2)
O Jesus, I Have Promised (verse 3)
O Little Town of Bethlehem (verse 3)
The Savior Calls, Let Every Ear
Softly and Tenderly Jesus Is Calling
This Is My Father's World
Whispering Hope
Whosoever Will

Secular Songs

The Bells of St. Mary's
Cheerful Little Earful
I Heard the Bells on Christmas Day
My Heart at Thy Sweet Voice
The Sound of Music
The Sound of Silence
Speak to Me of Love
Whispering
Winter Wonderland

Story

Read the story from a book titled *A Window to Heaven*, by Diane Komp (1992, pp. 42-44)—about a young man who saw and heard something analogous to "In the Garden."

Quotations

1. I have heard of thee by the hearing of the ear but now mine eye seeth thee.

Job 42:5 (KJV)

2. Mine ears hast thou opened.

Psalm 40:6 (KJV)

3. . . . and cut off his ear.

Matthew 26:51; Mark 14:47 (NKJV)

4. . . . and cut off his right ear.

Luke 22:50; John 18:10 (NKJV)

5. He who has an ear, let him hear.

Revelation 2:11, 29 (NIV)

6. . . . his ears are attentive to their cry.

Psalm 34:15 (NIV)

7. Friends, Romans, countrymen, lend me your ears.

William Shakespeare, Julius Caesar

Discussion

1. Are you a good listener? Do you have good hearing?
2. In the hymn "Softly and Tenderly Jesus Is Calling," where is He calling us to? Why is He calling us? Would you go? Are you ready to go?
3. How is your hearing? Is there a sound you can hear right now? What is it?
4. What kind of sounds do you like best (music, TV, birds singing, a babbling brook, the roar of the ocean)?
5. Do we learn better by seeing, doing, or listening?
6. Do you listen better now than when you were younger?
7. Discuss different "ear" expressions: up to his ears, giving an earful, bend one's ear, keep one's ear to the ground, I'm all ears,

my ears are burning, in one ear and out the other, out on one's ear, wet behind the ears. Also, eardrop, ear rot, earache, earshot, earflap, earplug, earmark, earpiercing, earsplitting.
8. Ear maladies include inner ear problems (dizziness) and my good ear (differential hearing); remedies for ear maladies are earphones, pocket talkers, and hearing aids.

Sensory Cues

1. Bring along a special effects tape with sounds for the group to recognize, such as farm animals or musical instruments.
2. Pass around an unusual-sounding instrument such as a bell tree at the start of the group. Encourage the members to explore its sounds.

Prayers

1. I don't know who—or what—put the question, I don't know when it was put. I don't even remember answering. But at some moment I did answer Yes to Someone—or Something—and from that hour I was certain that existence is meaningful and that, therefore, my life in self-surrender had a goal. From that moment I have known what it means "not to look back" and "to take no thought for the morrow."

> *Dag Hammarskjöld*
> *The Oxford Book of Prayer, p. 265*

2. Dear God, we pause to think of you in prayer. We close our eyes to pray with love in our hearts, for goodness and mercy all our days. We believe in the power of prayer to create joy in our lives. We pray in thanks and deep gratitude for all of our blessings. We pray for each one of us—for _____ *(name each person in the group one by one, something that you might do anytime you are doing a prayer. You might also pray for specific things for each group member, an approach we found effective in the past)*. Hear our prayer. Amen.

> *K. Kirkland*

HEART

Hymns

At the Name of Jesus (verse 4)
Create in Me a Clean Heart
The Day of Resurrection (verse 2)
Into My Heart
I've Found a Friend
Make Room Within My Heart, O God
Now Thank We All Our God
Thou Didst Leave Thy Throne and Thy Kingly Crown
When Morning Gilds the Skies
Where High the Heavenly Temple Stands (verse 5)

Secular Songs

Achy Breaky Heart
Heart and Soul
Heart of My Heart
Heartaches
I Left My Heart in San Francisco
My Foolish Heart
My Heart Will Go On
Peg O' My Heart
Stouthearted Men
Young at Heart

Story

A modified version of the story in Luke 24:13-35—the walk to Emmaus. This includes weariness of heart and later their hearts being "fired" (verse 32).

Discussion

1. Were you a heartbreaker? (It is surprising how often this draws a very positive response.)
2. How does it feel to have an aching/breaking heart?

3. What would it take to fix our hearts? The chorus of "Into My Heart" would be a natural sequel to this discussion.
4. Talk about Valentine's Day and its origins. Elicit memories of participating in giving and getting valentines.

Sensory Cues

1. There is a rich array of phrases and expressions related to the heart. If there are group members with some verbal dexterity, using word games can be fun, for example: My heart's not in it, heavyhearted, Put your heart into it, heart throb, a woman after my own heart, have a heart, She won their hearts, Bless your heart/Well, bless my heart, from the bottom of my heart, know it by heart, That did my heart good/warmed my heart, I don't have the heart to ask, My heart goes out to you, My heart sank/was in my boots, My heart was in my mouth, wears his heart on his sleeve, Eat your heart out. There's also heartless, sweetheart, heartbreaker, change of heart, heartache, and heartrending.
2. Have available valentines, or other heart-shaped items such as chocolates, a pillow, or even certain plant leaves.

Prayer

You made me for Yourself, and my heart is restless til it rests in You.

Saint Augustine
The Hodder Book of Christian Prayers
(Castle, 1986, p. 65)

LEGS AND FEET

Hymns

All God's Children Got Shoes
All the Way My Savior Leads Me
And Did Those Feet in Ancient Times
At Thy Feet, O Christ, We Lay
Battle Hymn of the Republic
God Be with You Till We Meet Again
How Beauteous Are Their Feet
I Got Shoes
In the Garden (refrain)
Just a Closer Walk with Thee
Lamp of Our Feet Whereby We Trace
Lead, Kindly Light
Morning Has Broken
O for a Closer Walk with God
O Master, Let Me Walk with Thee
O Thou Whose Feet Have Climbed Life's Hill
Praise, My Soul, the King of Heaven
Take My Life and Let It Be
Unto the Hills Around
Walk in the Light
We Walk by Faith and Not by Sight

Secular Songs

Charleston
Flat Foot Floogie
Heel and Toe Polka
I Could Have Danced All Night
Pennsylvania Polka
Save the Last Waltz for Me
Tiptoe Through the Tulips
The Varsity Drag
Walk Right In
You'll Never Walk Alone
Your Feet's Too Big

Stories

1. Read "Footprints" poem, with some suggestions for the non-ambulatory that God is carrying them now (as in "Swing low, sweet chariot, coming for to carry me home")
2. Jesus washing the disciples' feet—John 13
3. Acts 3:1-10—"feet and ankles became strong"

Quotations

1. Lest thou dash thy foot against a stone.

Psalm 91:12 (KJV)

2. Thy word is a lamp unto my feet.

Psalm 119:105 (KJV)

3. How beautiful on the mountains are the feet of those who bring good news.

Isaiah 52:7 (NIV)

Discussion

1. Do things with the residents' feet (respectful of boundaries and knowing the individuals)—touching, stroking, tracing—eventually, if appropriate, massaging. Then ask questions that will draw attention to their feet.
2. Think of how many miles your feet have traveled.
3. Think of the heavy loads your feet have carried (if women are present, speak of their pregnancies).
4. What is the longest trek you have had to make?
5. Did your feet ever get sore? (If appropriate, massage their feet.)
6. Did you ever have corns, bunions, callouses? What did that feel like?
7. What is it like to put your feet in warm water?
8. Have you ever walked on hot sand? Pebbles? Cool grass? What about soft, oozing mud?
9. What's it like to run in your boots in the snow?
10. What's the nicest pair of shoes that you've ever had?

11. Do you like your feet?
12. Do you/did you like to go for walks?
13. Do you have strong legs? Were you a good runner?
14. Recount the story behind the hymn "In the Garden" (Osbeck, 1982, p. 125). Can we walk with the Lord?
15. What kind of shoes do you have on your feet?
16. Have a general discussion about the shoes people are wearing, as an awareness exercise.
17. Pass around a bronzed baby shoe. Did anyone ever have this done to one of her/his child's baby shoes?
18. Did/do you like to dance? Have you ever done the Charleston? A polka? The two-step? Do you like waltzing?
19. Discuss feet expressions: feet of clay, ball is at one's feet, have a foot in both camps, foot in the door, one foot in the grave, one's feet on the ground, my foot!, put one's foot down, put one's foot in it, underfoot, foothills, foot-and-mouth disease, footloose, footwork, footlights, foot-candle, foot plate.
20. Discuss activities involving feet: walking, dancing, kicking, running.
21. Name problems associated with our legs and feet: swollen/edema, corns, callouses, flat feet, sprains, arthritis, stubbed toe, ingrown toenail.

Sensory Cues

1. A bronzed baby shoe
2. Assorted unusual shoes
3. Try doing the "Hokey Pokey," "Looby Loo," or an adaptation.

Prayer

Lord, thank you for my feet that have carried me all my life and walked many miles. Thank you for those who care for my feet now, especially nurses and podiatrists (foot doctors). Thank you for the memories of what my feet enabled me to do. Thank you for the beauty of my feet.

H. McIlveen

LIGHT

Hymns

Christ Is the World's Light
Fairest Lord Jesus (verse 3)
Father, Who the Light This Day Out of Darkness Didst Create
Glory to Thee My God
Godlight
Holy Ghost, with Light Divine
I Am the Light of the World
I Heard the Voice of Jesus Say
I Want to Walk as a Child of the Light
I've Seen the Light
Jesus Bids Us Shine
Joyful, Joyful, We Adore Thee
Lead, Kindly Light
The Lord Is My Light
Now Fades All Earthly Splendor
O Christ, You Are the Light and Day
O Love That Will Not Let Me Go (verse 2)
O Radiant Light
Shine, Jesus, Shine
This Little Light of Mine

Secular Songs

Let the Sun Shine In
You Are My Sunshine
You Are the Sunshine of My Life (Stevie Wonder)
You Light Up My Life

Stories

1. Genesis 1-4
2. Discuss the history of Hanukkah, the Festival of Lights. Hanukkah usually falls in December and is celebrated for eight days. The Talmud tells how Judah Maccabee and his followers had

defeated the Syrian overlords in the year 165. They entered the Holy Temple in Jerusalem that the Syrians had defiled, cleansed it and rededicated it to the service of God. Hanukkah is a Hebrew term for dedication. They didn't have enough oil for the lamps but found a small vial of oil in one of the Temple chambers which normally would only last them one evening. Miraculously, it lasted for eight nights, enough time for them to find some new oil. Bring in a menorah to illustrate Hanukkah. There is also the song, "Hanukkah."
Source: "The History of Hannukah" (sic). Online. June 29, 1998. Available: *http://www.ort.org/ort/hanukkah/history.htm*

3. Diwali is also a festival of lights. Food and presents are exchanged between family and friends. Originally a Hindu festival, it goes back to the story of a prince, Lord Rama, who had been in exile for fourteen years along with his wife Seeta and his younger brother Lashman. His father and stepmother asked him to return to become king. He was welcomed by the people who lit diwas all over the streets. Sikhs celebrate Diwali because some 400 years ago their sixth guru, Guru Hargobind Ji, returned home. He also freed fifty-two kings with him who had been imprisoned in India. All of the city of Amristar and the Golden Temple were aglow with lights, fireworks, and celebrations. Today Sikhs the world over celebrate Diwali in the evening by praying to God for peace.
Source: Flora, Harpal. "Diwali." Online. June 29, 1998. Available: *http://www.greenchilli.mcmail.com/DIWALI.htm*

4. Saul's conversion, Acts 9 (especially verse 3)

5. Constantine's conversion, when he saw a cross of light. (See Kerr and Mulder, 1983, pp. 4-10.)

Discussion

1. Discuss the light in the room, the sunlight coming in, and watching a sunrise.

2. What would life be like without light? What does light do?

3. Talk about the role of light in creation.

4. Jesus said, "I am the light of the world." What does that mean to you?

Sensory Cue

Light a candle, votive, or oil lamp in the center of the circle. Dim the lights and darken the room.

Prayers

1. May the Lord bless you and keep you: the Lord make his face shine upon you, and be gracious to you. The Lord lift up his countenance upon you, and give you peace.

Numbers 6:24-26 (NKJV)

2. May the blessings of light be upon you, light without and light within, and in all your comings and goings, may you ever have a kindly greeting from them you meet along the road.

Traditional Irish Prayer

MEALS

Hymns

As We Break the Bread
Blest Feast of Love
Bread of Heaven
Bread of Heaven, On Thee We Feed
Bread of Life
Bread of the World in Mercy Broken
Break Thou the Bread of Life
God and Man at Table Are Sat Down
I Am the Bread of Life
The Lamb's High Banquet
Let Us Break Bread Together on Our Knees
Sons of God
Sweet Feast of Love Divine
Wc Gather Together to Ask the Lord's Blessing

Secular Songs

Hey, Good Lookin' ("Whatcha Got Cookin'?")
Hot Cross Buns
In the Shade of the Old Apple Tree
I've Been Working on the Railroad ("Someone's
    in the Kitchen with Dinah")
Lemon Tree
Molly Malone
Oranges and Lemons
The Peanut Song
Rum and Coca-Cola
Shortnin' Bread
Sing for Your Supper
Tea for Two
Yes, We Have No Bananas

Story

The Last Supper—Matthew 26:20-30

Quotation

> And God said, "Behold, I have given you every herb bearing seed which is upon the face of all the earth, and every tree, in which is the fruit of a tree yielding seed; to you it shall be for meat."
>
> *Genesis 1:29 (KJV)*

Discussion

1. Do you like to cook? Can you cook?
2. Have you ever made bread? How do you make it? Do you use water or milk?
3. Has anyone here ever churned butter?
4. What kind of food is your favorite (fruit, sweets, chicken, turkey, pie)?
5. Do you remember saying the blessing/grace before you ate?
6. When you were growing up did you help prepare dinner? What did you do?
7. Did you have a garden to pick vegetables from?

Sensory Cues

1. Bring in food items for the group to experience; they should have a distinct taste/scent to stimulate a response. You might choose foods that are personal favorites of theirs or of their ethnicity.
2. Bring in a loaf of freshly baked bread for them to smell and taste.

Prayer

> Be present at our table, Lord
> Be here and everywhere adored
> These morsels bless, and grant that we
> may feast in Paradise with Thee. Amen.

(May be sung to tune of "Doxology.")

Note

You might try a communion service, since it relates to the theme.

MUSIC

Hymns

Come, Let Us Join Our Cheerful Songs
God Reveals His Presence (verse 3)
God Who Touches Earth with Beauty (verse 5)
Good Christian Men, Rejoice and Sing
He Keeps Me Singing
Music in My Soul
O Sing a New Song to the Lord
O Sons and Daughters, Let Us Sing
Over My Head
Songs of Praise
Sunshine in My Soul (verse 2)
We Have Heard the Joyful Sound

Secular Songs

The Music Goes Round and Round
Music, Music, Music
Sing (sing a song)
Singin' in the Rain
The Sound of Music
You and the Night and the Music

Story

Paul and Silas in prison—Acts 16:22-31

Quotation

Music is God's gift to man, the only art of heaven given to earth, the only art of earth we take to heaven.

Walter Savage Landor

Discussion

1. What kind of music do you like? Classical? Country? Love songs? Hymns? Rock and roll?

2. What do you like about music?
3. It's been said that music is the language of heaven—would you agree? Why?
4. Do you/did you play an instrument? Piano? Organ? Harmonica?
5. Do you sing? Have you ever sung in a choir?
6. Did any of your brothers or sisters play a musical instrument? What about your parents?
7. Did you ever have sing-alongs around the piano when you were growing up?

Sensory Cues

1. Listen to some favorite recordings of hymns or classical music.
2. Pass around a unique percussion instrument or an unusual instrument from a particular culture for the group to examine.
3. Listen to two contrasting songs (one sad, one lively/happy) and explore the group's responses to them.

Prayers

1. Lord, thank you for the music that brings our souls closer to heaven. Thank you for the feelings and the memories it brings to us, especially the joy that fills us deep within. For all the sounds that touch our lives, we thank you Lord. Amen.

K. Kirkland

2. Tune me, O Lord, into one harmony with You,
one full responsive vibrant chord;
Unto Your praise, all love and melody,
Tune me, O Lord.

Christina Rosetti
The Hodder Book of Christian Prayers
(Castle, 1986, p. 136)

PAIN

Hymns

Be Still, My Soul
I Need Thee Every Hour (verse 3)
In the Cross of Christ I Glory
Kum By Yah
O Love That Will Not Let Me Go (verse 3)
The Old Rugged Cross
The Servant Song
There Is a Balm in Gilead
What a Friend We Have in Jesus
Where Cross the Crowded Ways of Life (verse 5)

Secular Songs

Are You Lonesome Tonight?
Heartaches
I Don't Hurt Anymore
Lean on Me
Your Cheatin' Heart

Stories

1. The Crucifixion
2. Hymn stories for "What a Friend We Have in Jesus" or "O Love That Will Not Let Me Go" (Osbeck, 1982, pp. 276-277; p. 189)
3. Read Tim Hansel's story in the book *You Gotta Keep Dancing* (Hansel, 1985), concerning physical pain.

Quotations

1. God whispers to us in our joys,
   speaks to us in our conscience
   and shouts to us in our pain.

C. S. Lewis

2. The level of our emotional pain is in direct proportion to how much we are covering up.

Tim Hansel
Through the Wilderness of Loneliness, p. 62

3. Life can be counted on to provide all the pain that any of us might need.

Sheldon Kopp
You Gotta Keep Dancing (Hansel, p. 15)

4. The Skin Horse to the Velveteen Rabbit: "When you're Real you don't mind being hurt."

Margery Williams, The Velveteen Rabbit

5. Pain and suffering produce a fork in the road.

Tim Hansel
You Gotta Keep Dancing, p. 97

6. (Pain) inevitably affects the lives of those closest to us. . . pain is a shared experience, whether we want it to be or not.

Tim Hansel
You Gotta Keep Dancing, p. 118

Discussion

1. How can we tell when someone is in pain? Demonstrate bodily pain response, such as after hitting one's thumb with a hammer, hitting one's funny bone, stubbing one's toe, having stomach cramps, a toothache, a headache, or a backache. What does one do (physically) in each of these instances?
2. Which is worse, physical/bodily pain or sadness pain? The hymn stories mentioned previously would fit well here.
3. What can we do about pain? What soothes pain? What are our physical and emotional analgesics?
4. Does God (or Jesus) feel pain?
5. Discuss pain expressions: what a pain, pain in the neck, pain-killer.

Sensory Cue

The deaf have a sign for Jesus. The middle finger of each hand is placed in the palm of the other: Jesus, the one with wounded hands.

Tim Hansel

Prayer

Lord Jesus,
You know what pain is like.
You know
the torture of the scourge upon Your back,
the sting of the thorns upon Your brow,
the agony of the nails in Your hands.
You know what I'm going through just now.
Help me
to bear my pain
gallantly, cheerfully, and patiently,
and help me to remember
that I will never be tried
above what I am able to bear
and that You are with me,
even in this valley of the deep dark shadow,
for love's sake. Amen.

William Barclay
The Hodder Book of Christian Prayers #806
(Castle, 1986, p. 227)

REST

Hymns

Be Not Afraid
Be Still and Know
Be Still, My Soul
Eternal Rest
The Haven of Rest
Heaven Is My Home (verse 3)
I Heard the Voice of Jesus Say
Jesus, I Am Resting, Resting
Jesus Will Give You Rest
O Day of Rest and Gladness
O Lord of Life (verse 4)
There Is a Place of Quiet Rest
This Alone

Secular Songs

Brahms' Lullaby
Cruising Down the River
The 59th Street Bridge Song (Feelin' Groovy)
Hush Little Baby (The Mockingbird)
It's Only a Shanty
Sweet and Low
(There'll Be Bluebirds Over) the White Cliffs of Dover
The West, a Nest, and You, Dear (Mort Kenny
    and His Western Gentlemen)

Quotation

> Come unto me, all ye that labour and are heavy laden, and I
> will give you rest.
>
> *Matthew 11:28 (KJV)*

Discussion

1. There is something very inviting when Jesus says, "Come unto
   me and I will give you rest." What does "rest" mean to you?
   Do you yearn to rest?

2. God rested on the seventh day. What did you do on Sundays when you were growing up?
3. For those who are busy/agitated all the time, ask what they do to relax or during leisure time. Are you able to rest? When do you take some time out for just you?

Sensory Cues

1. Images of restful scenes
2. Listening to a soothing piece of classical music
3. Guided visualization

Prayer

> O Lord, support us all the day long of this troublous life until the shadows lengthen and the evening comes, and the busy world is hushed, and the fever of life is over, and our work is done. Then Lord, in your mercy grant us a safe lodging and holy rest, and peace at the last. Amen.

The Hodder Book of Christian Prayers
(Castle, 1986, pp. 230-231)

SCENT/SMELL (NOSE)

Hymns

There are very few hymns that refer to a sense of smell, although some hymns about nature refer to flowers and other fragrances:

Crown Him with Many Crowns (verse 3)
Fairest Lord Jesus
For the Beauty of the Earth
Morning Has Broken
O Worship the King, All Glorious Above

The Christmas carol "The First Noel" speaks about myrrh and frankincense, which are very aromatic. The hymn "Crown Him with Many Crowns" tells of "fair flowers of paradise that extend their fragrance ever sweet." "In the garden" may be a good stepping stone to remembering the scents of flowers.

Secular Songs

April Showers
Bluebells of Scotland
I'll Be with You in Apple Blossom Time
Java Jive
Jeannine, I Dream of Lilac Time
Lemon Tree
My Wild Irish Rose
Red Roses for a Blue Lady
Rose of Tralee
Shoo Fly Pie and Apple Pan Dowdy
Shortnin' Bread
Sweet Violets
Tea for Two
Tip Toe Through the Tulips

Story

Isaac, who was blind, tried valiantly to identify which son had come by his sense of smell—Genesis 27, especially verse 27

Discussion

1. We use "props" here liberally: cooking aromas (vanilla, vinegar, freshly ground coffee); medical odors (liniment such as Absorbine Junior); flowers, incense, sulfur, aftershave lotion, cigars—anything strongly scented. Essential oils are wonderful too. Essential oil of peppermint can be stimulating. Use the scents to test their ability to smell and to awaken associations between the aromas and the world of memories.
2. What are your favorite smells? (With a nonverbal group, you may have to suggest some attractive smells.)
3. What detective work do we do with our noses (smelling smoke when there is a fire, discovering spoiled food in our refrigerator, sniffing out freshly baked bread)?
4. When might someone try to trick our sense of smell (e.g., when someone who is drinking alcohol tries to hide it with another odor; when, as a boy, I tried to hide from my mother that I had been smoking)?
5. You can introduce the story about Isaac after this discussion.
6. Nose expressions: he has a nose for scandal or lying, nose around, nose out/win by a nose, get up a person's nose, keep one's nose clean, put one's nose out of joint, turn up one's nose at something, right under one's nose, keep your nose to the grindstone, with one's nose in the air, cut off his nose to spite his face, nosedive, nosegay, nosy, noseband (lower band of a bridle passing over the horse's nose), nosebag.

Sensory Cues

1. Bring a dog into the group for them to pet. Discuss a dog's keen sense of smell.
2. Use the different items mentioned in Secular Songs to stimulate responses and memories.

Prayer

Lord God, thank you for the many wonderful fragrant things in this world. Thank you for noses than can smell. Thank you that you refer to us in our obedience to you as being like a "lovely aroma" in your nostrils. May we continue to give you pleasure. We ask this for your glory. Amen.

H. McIlveen

Note

The sense of smell can be lost as a result of some forms of dementia.

SIGHT (EYES)

Hymns

Abide with Me (verse 5)
Battle Hymn of the Republic
Be Not Afraid
Be Thou My Vision
Beneath the Cross of Jesus (verse 2)
Beyond the Sunset
Fairest Lord Jesus
Fill All My Vision, Savior, I Pray
Give Us, O God, the Grace to See
God Sees the Little Sparrow Fall (He Loves Me Too)
His Eye Is on the Sparrow
In the Twinkling of an Eye
Jesus, These Eyes Have Never Seen
Just as I Am, Without One Plea
Look and Live
My Faith Looks Up to Thee
Nobody Knows the Trouble I've Seen
The Old Rugged Cross
Open My Eyes, That I May See
Open Our Eyes, Lord
Sun of My Soul, Thou Savior Dear (verses 1, 2)
Unto the Hills Around
We See Not the Way
We Would See Jesus

Secular Songs

Beautiful Brown Eyes
Don't It Make My Brown Eyes Blue
Green Eyes
I Only Have Eyes for You
Jeepers, Creepers
Oh, What a Beautiful Mornin'
Smoke Gets in Your Eyes

The Star-Spangled Banner ("O, say can you see . . . ")
When Irish Eyes Are Smiling

Stories

1. The healing of a blind man—Mark 8:22-26
2. 2 Kings 6:11-19
3. Mark 8:22-26
4. Luke 24:13-35
5. The story of Helen Keller or other famous blind people such as Ray Charles, Roy Orbison, Stevie Wonder, Italian tenor Andrea Bocelli

Quotations

1. A man falls in love through his eyes, a woman through her ears.

   Woodrow Wyatt, 1981

2. Open my eyes that I may behold . . .

   Psalm 119:18 (KJV)

3. . . . thine eyes beheld my inborn substance.

   Psalm 139:16 (KJV)

4. . . . eye is the lamp of your body.

   Luke 11:34 (NIV)

5. . . . now my eye sees you.

   Job 42:5 (NKJV)

Discussion

1. Comment on the residents' eyes, their color and characteristics. Acknowledge that sometimes we have difficulty seeing. Wear a pair of glasses; see if the group members can tell you what they are. Look in their eyes up close so that, if possible, you can establish eye contact. Try using body language (e.g., blinking, winking, frowning, raising your eyebrows, squinting); the

group members may themselves communicate in some of these ways.

2. Can we tell if people are sad or happy or mischievous by looking into their eyes?
3. What does the expression "The eyes are the windows of the soul" mean to you? What else can we tell when we look at people's eyes? What does it mean when their eyes are downcast or when they won't look at us?
4. What flows/comes out of our eyes? Could we live without tears? How do tears help us?
5. If God had eyes like ours, what would they look like? Is that how He looks at you?
6. What color are your eyes?
7. Do you wear glasses? Do you remember when you got your first pair of glasses?
8. How important is eyesight? What's it like to have poor eyesight or blindness? How do you manage? What do you do differently?
9. Discuss the meaning of the line "was blind but now I see," in "Amazing Grace."
10. Does God watch over us (parallel to "His Eye Is on the Sparrow")?
11. Discuss sight expressions: on a clear day, you can see forever; what a sight for sore eyes, hawkeye, eye for an eye, have an eye for something, keep an eye on, keep an eye open/out for, keep your eyes peeled, look someone in the eye, in a pig's eye, "my eye," seeing eye to eye, with one's eyes wide open, up to the eyeballs, eyeball-to-eyeball, eye level, eyesore, eyetooth, lie our eyes, in the eye of the beholder, there's more to this than meets the eye, the eye of the storm.
12. Discuss eye problems such as cataracts, blindness, and redness.

Sensory Cues

1. Discuss how people connect with each other by making eye contact. At the start of the group, encourage them to make eye contact and shake hands with their neighbors and the other group members.

2. Discuss the hymn "Beyond the Sunset," which was inspired by a blind man who said he could see "beyond the sunset" (Osbeck, 1985, pp. 48-49).

Prayers

1. Lord, we give thanks today for our sight and our insight, for the lifetime of experiences our eyes have witnessed. When my eyesight is weak and dim, Lord, be my vision. Just as your eye is on the sparrow, we know and comfort that your eye is on us also. We give our thanks in Jesus' name, Amen.

H. McIlveen

2. From the hymn "Open my eyes that I may see," which may also be sung.

> Open my eyes that I may see
> Glimpses of truth Thou hast for me;
> Place in my hands the wonderful key
> That shall unclasp and set me free.
> Silently now I wait for Thee,
> Ready, my God, Thy will to see;
> Open my eyes, illumine me,
> Spirit Divine!

VOICE (MOUTH)

Hymns

Glorious Things of Thee Are Spoken
God Hath Spoken by His Prophets
Hark, the Voice of Jesus Calling
Hark, the Voice of Love and Mercy
I Heard the Voice of Jesus Say
I Hear Thy Welcome Voice
I'll Praise My Maker While I've Breath
Lift Your Glad Voices
O for a Thousand Tongues to Sing
Open My Eyes, That I May See (verse 3)
Speak, Lord, in the Stillness
The Voice of God Is Calling
Wonderful Words of Life

Secular Songs

I Believe in Music
I'd Like to Teach the World to Sing
Lift Every Voice
Sing
Speak to Me of Love
Whispering
Whispering Hope

Stories

1. The young nineteen-year-old who had a vision of a man who spoke with him and walked with him in a garden. (See Komp, pp. 42-44.) This story relates to the hymn "In the Garden."
2. From the same book, the story of the five-year-old with cancer who asked her parents if they could hear the angels singing. She died momentarily after that. (See Komp, 1992, p. 28.)
3. Play an excerpt of a famous singer such as Nelson Eddy, Frank Sinatra, Billy Holiday, or Ella Fitzgerald, and see if the group

can identify who it is by the person's voice. Tell some biographical information about the singer and elicit any memories/associations the group has of that person.

Quotation

If anyone hears my voice and opens the door, I will come in . . .

Revelation 3:20 (NIV)

Discussion

1. Have you noticed how everyone's speaking voice is unique.
2. Do you remember the sound of your mother's voice? Your father's?
3. Do you like to sing?
4. Did you ever sing in a choir?
5. Would you say you have a good singing voice? (See Note.)

Sensory Cue

Prepare a tape of some of the group members talking and play it for them. See if they recognize their own voice or the voices of other people in the group.

Prayer

Thank you, Lord, for our voices so that we may pray and talk to you; for our voices that express themselves and sing with joy. Thank you for your voice which brought us the light of the world and the Word of God. We lift up our voices to you in thanks. Amen.

H. McIlveen

Note

Many people were told in their early childhood that they can't/ shouldn't sing. Take time to undo this. Give realistic/appropriate praise for their singing. I use different responses when they put down their singing voices, including asking who told them that in the first place. I say things such as "Well, you sound fine to me, and I'm glad you come here every week to sing with us," or "If you're singing and enjoying yourself, that's what's important." A compliment, especially from a musician, is meaningful, self-esteem building, and usually well-received.

WEARINESS/FATIGUE

Hymns

A Shelter in the Time of Storm
Are You Weary, Heavy Laden?
Art Thou Weary, Art Thou Troubled?
Beneath the Cross of Jesus
Come Unto Me, Ye Weary
Hark, Hark, My Soul (verse 2)
His Yoke Is Easy, His Burden Is Light
I Heard the Voice of Jesus Say
Jesus, Refuge of the Weary
Lead Me Home (words and music by Denny Correll)
Like a River Glorious
Nobody Knows the Trouble I've Seen
Rock of Ages, Cleft for Me
Softly and Tenderly Jesus Is Calling
What a Friend We Have in Jesus

Secular Songs

Just A-Wearyin' for You
Keep Right on to the End of the Road
Ol' Man River
Show Me the Way to Go Home
Sleepy Time Gal
Two Sleepy People

Story

Tell the story behind the hymn "Beneath the Cross of Jesus" (Osbeck, 1982, p. 39).

Quotations

1. Come unto me all you who are weary and burdened, and I will give you rest. Take my yoke upon you and learn from me, for I am gentle and humble in heart, and you will find rest for your souls. For my yoke is easy and my burden is light.

   Matthew 11:28-30 (NIV)

2. They shall not grow old, as we that are left grow old:
   Age shall not weary them, nor the years condemn.
   At the going down of the sun and in the morning
   We will remember them.

Laurence Binyon, 1914, "For the Fallen"

3. Here is the answer which I will give to President Roosevelt . . .
   We shall not fail or falter; we shall not weaken or tire. Neither
   the sudden shock of battle nor the long-drawn trials of vigilance
   and exertion will wear us down. Give us the tools and we will
   finish the job.

Winston Churchill, February 9, 1941

Discussion

1. Do you get tired? What makes you tired?
2. How do you feel when you've worked a long, long time?
3. When you're tired, do you get grumpy? Cranky?
4. Where would you like to be when you're tired?
5. Who would you like to be there to help you when you're tired?

Sensory Cue

Demonstrate with an easy chair the usual way of sitting that is
characteristic of a weary person or someone yawning.

Prayer

O Lord, support us all the day long of this troublous life, until
the shadows lengthen and the evening comes, the busy world
is hushed, the fever of life is over, and our work is done. Then,
Lord, in your mercy, grant us safe lodging, a holy rest, and
peace at last. Amen.

Cardinal Newman
The Hodder Book of Christian Prayers
(Castle, 1986, pp. 230-231)

Special Occasions

COMMUNION

Hymns

As He Gathered at His Table
As We Break the Bread
Bread of Heaven, on Thee We Feed
Bread of the World in Mercy Broken
Break Thou the Bread of Life
Come, Share the Lord; O Living Bread from Heaven
God and Man at Table Are Sat Down
I Am the Bread of Life (and I will raise him up)
In Christ There Is No East or West
Let Us Break Bread Together on Our Knees
May the Light (David Roth)
Sing a New Song to the Lord

Secular Songs

The More We Get Together
Peace Is (Fred Small)

Stories

1. John 6:35,37
2. Luke 22:7-20 (excerpt)

Discussion

1. Do you remember receiving Communion at church?
2. What is Communion about?

3. What does Communion mean to you?
4. What does the bread symbolize or mean?
5. What does the wine symbolize or mean?
6. Do you remember your first Communion?

Sensory Cue

Bring bread and wine for the Communion rite: demonstrate with the breaking of bread and pouring of wine.

Prayer

On You we cast our care; we live through You, who know'st our every need: O feed us with Your grace, and give our souls this day the living bread. Amen.

John Wesley
The Hodder Book of Christian Prayers
(Castle, 1986, p. 291)

Note

The ritual of Communion is more important than the questions about remembering or interpreting it. Depending on the cognitive abilities of your group, it may be better to perform the service and the Communion ritual.

EASTER

Hymns

All Shall Be Well
Christ Arose
Christ Is Alive
Christ the Lord Is Risen Again
Christ the Lord Is Risen Today
Crown Him with Many Crowns
The Day of Resurrection
Easter Song
He Lives Who Once Was Dead
I Am the Resurrection
I Know That My Redeemer Lives
Joy Dawned Again on Easter Day
Just a Closer Walk with Thee
The Old Rugged Cross
Sing a New Song to the Lord
The Strife Is O'er, the Battle Done

Secular Songs

Easter Parade
Eggbert, the Easter Egg
Here Comes Peter Cottontail

Story

Jesus appears to Mary Magdalene—John 20:10-18

Discussion

1. What does Easter mean to you?
2. What was the saddest moment of your life?
3. When someone is sad how can we help—by asking them what's wrong or by taking an interest in them personally?
4. What do we mean when we say, "It's too good to be true"?

5. Have you had an experience when something was "too good to be true"?
6. What does Christ's death and resurrection mean for us?

Sensory Cues

1. One possible approach is for the two leaders to role-play some inadequate responses to sadness and then role-play a response that reflects Jesus' approach to Mary Magdalene.
2. Bring in some hot cross buns for the group to enjoy with coffee following the session. See what memories are evoked by the sharing of these buns.

Prayers

1. Lord, You who turned Magdalene's sorrow into joy, come alive within my experience, within my sadness, disappointments, and doubts. Come alive as the peace and assurance that nothing can kill. Amen.

H. McIlveen

2.   The Lord Is Risen

>   Sing, soul of mine, this day of days,
>   The Lord is risen.
>   Toward the sun-rising set thy face,
>   The Lord is risen.
>   Behold He giveth strength and grace;
>   For darkness, light; for mourning, praise;
>   For sin, His holiness; for conflict, peace.
>   Arise, O soul, this Easter Day!
>   Forget the tomb of yesterday,
>   For thou from bondage art set free;
>   Thou sharest in His victory
>   And life eternal is for thee,
>   Because the Lord is risen.

Author Unknown
(Edward MacHugh's Treasury
of Gospel Hymns and Poems, 1938)

FATHER (FATHER'S DAY)

Hymns

Abba, Father
Be Thou My Vision
Can a Little Child Like Me?
Children of the Heavenly Father
Come Let Us Sing of a Wonderful Love
Eternal Father, Strong to Save
Faith of Our Fathers
Father Eternal, Lord of the Ages
Father, in Whom We Live
Father, Mercy
Father Most Holy, Merciful, and Tender
Father of Heaven, Whose Love Profound
Glory Be to the Father
How Strong and Sweet My Father's Care
In the Sweet By-and-By
Jesus Loves Even Me
Lavish Love, Abundant Beauty
Praise, My Soul, the King of Heaven
The Prodigal Son
Sing Praise to the Father
This Is My Father's World
We All Believe in One True God
We Thank Thee, Loving Father
Whosoever Will

Secular Songs

Cat's in the Cradle (Harry Chapin)
The Green, Green Grass of Home
Just a Baby's Prayer at Twilight
Lemon Tree
The Living Years
When Father Papered the Parlor

Story

The father in the story of the Prodigal Son—Luke 15:11-32

Sensory Cue

If possible, bring photos of the group members' fathers.

Discussion

1. What do you remember about your father?
2. What was (or for some, *is*) he like?
3. Do you look like your father?
4. What did he do for a living?
5. For those who are aware that their father has died, do they remember his death and how they handled it?
6. In what ways are you like your father? For males, what kind of father were (are) you?
7. Talk about our Father in heaven.

Prayer

Our Father who art in heaven, hallowed be Thy name, Thy kingdom come, Thy will be done on earth as it is in heaven. Give us this day our daily bread, and forgive our trespasses as we forgive those who trespass against us; and lead us not into temptation, but deliver us from evil. For Thine is the kingdom, the power, and the glory, forever and ever, Amen.

The Lord's Prayer

GIFTS (SECOND ADVENT)

Hymns

All That I Am
All That I Need
All Things Bright and Beautiful
Be Thou My Vision
Behold the Amazing Gift of Love
Can a Little Child Like Me?
Canticle of the Gift
Giver of the Perfect Gift
No, Not One! (verse 5)
O That Will Be Glory (verse 2)
This Day God Gives Me
When Two or More

Christmas/Gift-Related Songs

All Good Gifts (from *Godspell*)
As with Gladness Men of Old (verse 3)
Count Your Blessings
The Friendly Beasts
The Huron Carol
In the Bleak Mid-Winter (verse 4)
The Little Drummer Boy
Mary, Dear Mother of Jesus
O Come, Little Children
O Little Town of Bethlehem
We Three Kings

Story

The gifts brought by the Magi—Matthew 2:1-11

Quotation

Every good gift and every perfect gift is from above, and cometh down from the Father of lights, with whom is no variableness, neither shadow of turning.

James 1:17 (KJV)

Discussion

1. What was the best gift you've ever received?
2. Did you always get what you wished for?
3. Is it better to give or to receive?
4. What gifts can you give that money can't buy?

Sensory Cues

1. Distribute small gifts for the residents.
2. Bring in a beautifully wrapped box of assorted sweets, cookies, or chocolates to be passed around the group.

Prayers

1. What can I give Him, Poor as I am? If I were shepherd, I would bring a lamb, If I were a Wise Man I would do my part—yet what can I give Him—give my heart.

Christina Rosetti

2. Lord Jesus Christ, take all my freedom, my memory, my understanding, and my will. All that I have and cherish,You have given me. I surrender it all to be guided by Your will. Your grace and your love are wealth enough for me. Give me these, Lord Jesus, and I ask for nothing more.

Ignatius of Loyola
The Hodder Book of Christian Prayers
(Castle, 1986, p. 93)

3. Dear Lord, we come to this gathering to give thanks to You for the many gifts to us. We acknowledge You as the giver of all gifts, not only those which feed and clothe our bodies but also those which bring extra joy and richness into our lives. We thank You most of all for the joy of fellowship and we ask You to bless us as we meet here together this day. Amen.

(Source: Rodeheaver et al. (Eds.), 1934, p. 262)

HOPE/WAITING (THIRD ADVENT)

Hymns

Abide with Me
All My Hope on God Is Founded
Angels from the Realms of Glory
Battle Hymn of the Republic
Beneath the Cross of Jesus
Christ Arose
Give to the Winds Your Fears
God Is My Great Desire
Help Us Accept Each Other
Hope of the World
In a Monastery Garden
It Came Upon the Midnight Clear
It Is No Secret What God Can Do
Jesus, Savior, Pilot Me
Lead, Kindly Light
Lead On, O King Eternal
Looking for that Blessed Hope
Lord of All Hopefulness
My Faith Looks Up to Thee
Now Thank We All Our God
O God, Our Help in Ages Past
O Little Town of Bethlehem
Softly and Tenderly Jesus Is Calling
Something Worth Living For
Soon and Very Soon
Teach Me Lord, to Wait
When with Waiting Long

Secular Songs

Bridge Over Troubled Water
Gracias a la Voda (Videta Para)
Keep Right on to the End of the Road
Land of Hope and Glory

New World Coming
(There'll Be Bluebirds Over) the White Cliffs of Dover
Tomorrow
Wait Till the Sun Shines, Nellie
Where the Blue of the Night Meets the Gold of the Day
Whispering Hope

Stories

1. The story of Abraham and Sarah waiting for the son that God promised them—Genesis 18:1-15, 21:1-7
2. People waiting for a Savior—Luke 2:22-35, 2:36-38
3. The story behind the writing of the hymn "Abide with Me" (Osbeck, 1982, p. 16)
4. The story behind the writing of the carol "Angels from the Realms of Glory" (Osbeck, 1982, p. 32)

Discussion

1. Are you hopeful about tomorrow?
2. Have you ever hoped for something and had it come true (marriage, children, a good job, a gift, travel, better health)? What does it mean to "give up hope"? What does it mean when a situation is hopeless? How does it feel when things are hopeless? When have you felt the most hopeless?
3. Did you ever give up hope, only to have your hope rekindled? What do you do when things seem hopeless?
4. Does the desire to die increase as you get older? Some people say, "I'm useless and not needed anymore," or "I am no good for anything anymore."
5. Is it sometimes appropriate to acknowledge that hope is gone?
6. They say that good things come to those who wait. What does that mean? How is that true?
7. What awaits us after we die?
8. Discuss the hymn "Softly and Tenderly Jesus is Calling," in which Jesus is waiting and watching for you and me to come home.
9. Mention some waiting expressions: a watched pot never boils, this can't wait, wait upon someone, wait up, lie in wait for, wait

out, waiting list, waiting room. These are also things we wait for: Christmas, summer holidays, to grow up, for an important letter. Do you remember waiting for Christmas Day to arrive?
10. Why is waiting so difficult? What helps our waiting?
11. List some hope expressions: hoping against hope, not a hope on earth, some hope, hope chest, young hopeful, hopeless case. "Hope springs eternal in the human breast" (Alexander Pope); "While the sick man has life, there is hope" (Cicero); "All we can do is hope and pray."

Sensory Cues

1. An hourglass
2. A calendar with an upcoming occasion circled

Prayer

O God who has folded back the mantle of the night to clothe us in the golden glory of the day, chase from our hearts all gloomy thoughts, and make us glad with the brightness of hope, that we may effectively aspire to unwon virtues: through Jesus Christ Our Lord, Amen.

Ancient Collect
The Hodder Book of Christian Prayers
(Castle, 1986, pp. 110-111)

LOVE (FOURTH ADVENT)

Hymns

Blessed Assurance, Jesus Is Mine (verse 3)
Come, Let Us Sing of a Wonderful Love
God in His Love for Us
Help Us to Help Each Other, Lord
I Never Felt Such Love in My Soul Before (old spiritual)
Jesus, Lover of My Soul
Jesus Loves Even Me
Jesus Loves Me
Love Divine, All Loves Excelling
Love Lifted Me
My Song Is Love Unknown
The Ninety and Nine
O the Deep, Deep, Love of Jesus
O Love That Will Not Let Me Go
O Perfect Love, All Human Thought Transcending
Peace Is Flowing Like a River
Peace Prayer
Ubi Caritas
Whatsoever You Do to the Least of My Brothers

Secular Songs

Almost every song is about love in one fashion or another; choose some standard ones or personal favorites of those in the group.

All You Need Is Love
Have I Told You Lately That I Love You?
I Love You Truly
Let Me Call You Sweetheart
Love Me Tender
May Love Surround You

Stories

1. The parable of the Prodigal Son—Luke 15:11-32
2. The parable of the Good Samaritan—Luke 10:25-37

Poem

Love

When one loves, and love meets no return,
There is no pain, that in the heart can burn,
More bitterly unquenched by tears,
And smouldering lie through dreary years—
Like love unloved.

When one loves, and love meets warm return,
There is no joy, which in the heart can yearn,
Will make the world so beautiful, so fair,
As when love's incense fills the air—
When love is loved.

Minnie A. Dawson
(Hamlyn, 1932, p. 15)

Quotations

1. Love is patient, love is kind. It does not envy, it does not boast, it is not proud. It is not rude, it is not self-seeking, it is not easily angered, it keeps no record of wrongs. Love does not delight in evil, but rejoices with the truth. It always protects, always trusts, always hopes, always perseveres. Love never fails.

   I Corinthians 13:4-8 (NIV)

2. God is love, and he who abide in love abides in God, and God in him.

   John 4:16 (NKJV)

Discussion

1. When you love someone, what shows that you love them?
2. How do you like people to show their love for you?

3. When is it difficult to love someone?
4. When is it difficult for someone else to love you?
5. What's the best thing about love?
6. How does God show that He loves us?

Sensory Cue

Pass a red rose around the group at the beginning of the session (make sure there are no thorns) for the people to smell and touch. Associate the rose with love.

Prayer

Pray God make all bad people good, and all good people nice.

Child's Prayer

MEMORIES OF CHRISTMAS

Hymns

Any selection of familiar carols

Secular Songs

There are also many popular Christmas songs of a nonreligious nature, such as:

Deck the Halls with Boughs of Holly
Jingle Bells
Jolly Old Saint Nicholas
The Twelve Days of Christmas
We Wish You a Merry Christmas

Stories

1. The story of the angels appearing to the shepherds
2. The story of the shepherds finding the Christ child

Discussion

1. What comes to mind when you think of Christmas? What is your best Christmas memory? Your worst?
2. Did you spend Christmas with family? Was there a lot of cooking? Did you bake?
3. Do you remember a special Christmas present you were given (or gave)?
4. Do you remember what Christmas was like when you were six years old?
5. What decorations do/did you as a family do?
6. Did you ever chop down your own Christmas tree?

Sensory Cues

1. Use a creche/manger scene for the telling of the shepherds finding the Christ child.

2. Set up a yuletide log with holly on it and a candle burning in the center.

Prayers

1. This can be recited or sung:

> Into my heart, in my heart
> Into my heart, Lord Jesus
> Come in today
> Come in to stay
> Come into my heart, Lord Jesus.

from the hymn "Into My Heart"
by Harry D. Clarke
(Choice Hymns of the Faith, p. 50)

2. O holy child of Bethlehem, be born in us today.
Let us so live that others may know
we have invited you to dwell with us
and to share our homes, our work,
and every activity that claims our time.
With gratitude for the wonderful gift, we ask it. Amen.

(Source: Rodeheaver et al. (Eds.), 1934, p. 268)

MOTHER (MOTHER'S DAY)

Hymns

Ave Maria (Bach/Gounod or Schubert)
The God Whom Earth and Sea and Sky
I Would Be True
Mother (words and music by Nona G. Croxford)
My Mother's Prayer
Sometimes I Feel Like a Motherless Child
Sweetest Mother
Take This Message to Mother
Tell Mother I'll be There

Secular Songs

Always Take Mother's Advice
Did Your Mother Come from Ireland?
Dreaming of Home and Mother
I Want a Girl Just Like the Girl that Married Dear Old Dad
Let It Be
Ma, He's Making Eyes At Me!
M-O-T-H-E-R
Mother Machree
My Mother's Old Red Shawl
Songs My Mother Taught Me
That Wonderful Mother of Mine

Stories

1. Mary, mother of Jesus—having/giving birth to a child who was unusual; worried about her son's activity/trying to protect him; watching him die
2. The story of Hanna wanting to become a mother, then finally having a child and giving him up—Samuel 1:2

Poem

The noblest thoughts my soul can claim,
The holiest words my tongue can frame,
Unworthy are to praise the name
More sacred than all other.

An infant when her love first came—
A man, I find it just the same;
Reverently I breathe her name,
The blessed name of mother.

(Source: Rodeheaver et al. (Eds.), 1934, p. 265)

Discussion

1. Why are mothers important?
2. Tell us about your mother. What was (is) she like? Did she work? What did she do?
3. Are you like your mother? Do you take after/look like her?
4. What's your fondest memory of her? (This may be difficult for some people who were not close to their mother. You may need to explore: how would you have liked her to be?)
5. Imagine that she's in the room right now: what would you say to her?
6. What kind of mother are/were you?
7. How does a mother feel/cope if her child dies? (This may be a more common experience than you imagine). How do you cope? You might parallel the discussion to the feelings and actions of Mary when Jesus was crucified.

Sensory Cues

1. If possible, bring photos of the group members' mothers.
2. An alternative could be photos of the mothers in the group with their children.

Prayers

1. Hail Mary, full of grace, the Lord is with thee. Blessed art thou among women, and blessed is the fruit of Thy womb, Jesus. Holy Mary, Mother of God, pray for us sinners, now and at the hour of our death. Amen.

Traditional Catholic Prayer

2. Dear Lord, as we remember our mothers today, we ask that you fill our hearts with love and warm memories, that we may cherish all that she was able to do and provide for us. For all her goodness, the things we learned from her and because of her, we thank you Lord. Amen.

H. McIlveen

Note

Be sensitive to the fact that some women could not bear children, and this may be embarrassing or difficult for them to talk about. Some also chose not to have children, and some never married. It's very important to be respectful of the choices people made in their lives and not to suggest that they "missed the boat" by not marrying or not having children.

PROMISES (FIRST ADVENT)

Hymns

Blessed Assurance, Jesus Is Mine
Blest Be the God of Israel
How Firm a Foundation
I'll Praise My Maker
Jesus Lives and So Shall I
O Jesus, I Have Promised
O that Will Be Glory
Open My Eyes, That I May See
Soon and Very Soon
Standing on the Promises
Tell Out, My Soul, the Greatness of the Lord
There's a Quiet Understanding
There's a Rainbow Shining Somewhere
When the Roll is Called Up Yonder
Whosoever Will (verse 3)
Wonderful Words of Life

Secular Songs

I Beg Your Pardon (I Never Promised You a Rose Garden)
    (Johnny Burnette)
I'll Be Seeing You (Liberace)
O Promise Me

Stories

1. The promise of Christ's coming
2. Jesus' promise to the thief on the cross—"I tell you the truth, today you will be with me in paradise."—Luke 23:43 (NIV)

Quotations

1. And God shall wipe away all tears from their eyes; and there shall be no more death, neither sorrow, nor crying, neither shall there be any more pain; for the former things are passed away.

Revelation 21:4 (KJV)

2. I thought of him as a young man of promise [Churchill]. Now I see that he is a man of promises.

Lord Balfour

3. I never promised you a rose garden.

Hannah Green, "Rose Garden"

4. Well, I don't know what will happen now. We've been to the mountain top. I won't mind. Like anybody, I would like to have a long life. Longevity has its place. But I'm not concerned about that now. I just want to do God's will. And He's allowed me to go up to the mountain. And I've looked over, and I've seen the promised land. I may not get there with you, but I want you to know tonight that we as a people will get to the promised land. So I'm happy tonight. I'm not worried about anything. I'm not fearing any man. Mine eyes have seen the glory of the coming of the Lord.

Martin Luther King Jr.,
April 3, 1968, Memphis, TN

5. Vote for the man who promises least; he'll be the least disappointing.

Bernard Baruch

6. The woods are lovely, dark and deep,
   but I have promises to keep,
   and miles to go before I sleep,
   and miles to go before I sleep.

Robert Frost
"Stopping by Woods on a Snowy Evening"

7. I shall return.

General Douglas MacArthur

8. A promise made is a debt unpaid.

Robert Service
(from the poem "The Cremation of Sam McGee")

Discussion

1. Has anyone ever had someone break a promise made to him/her?

2. How do broken promises affect us?
3. Has anyone made promises and not kept them?
4. If you could make any promise or wish come true, what would it be?
5. What do you think God's promise is for us?
6. Some individuals have a background that has exposed them to the scriptures. You might try reciting a well-known verse, seeing if the individual can recite the remainder along with you, for example "God so loved the world . . . " (John 3:16).
7. Promise expressions: promised land, promising, promissory note, promising beginning, promising career, I promised myself.

Sensory Cue

Pass around a picture or drawing of a rainbow and discuss it as a symbol of God's promise, his covenant.

Prayer

Come unto me all of you that labour and are heavy laden and I will give you rest. Take my yoke upon you, and learn of me; for I am meek and lowly in heart: and ye shall find rest unto your souls. For my yoke is easy, and my burden is light.

Matthew 11:28-30 (KJV)

RENEWAL/NEW YEAR'S DAY

Hymns

Behold the Tabernacle
Count Your Blessings
It's a Brand New Day
Morning Has Broken
Renew Me, O Eternal Light
Sing a New Song to the Lord
Standing by a Purpose True
Standing on the Promises
This Is the Day
With Heart Renewed

Secular Songs

Auld Lang Syne
Happy New Year
Starting Over
Tomorrow
Turn, Turn, Turn
When It's Springtime in the Rockies

Story

The reinstatement of Peter—John 21:15-19

Discussion

1. Have you ever wanted to make a "fresh start"? Did you?
2. What renews your faith (e.g., singing hymns, attending church, praying)?
3. Have you ever made a New Year's resolution? What?
4. If you made a resolution today, what would it be?

Sensory Cue

Plant a flower seedling.

Prayers

1. O God in heaven, renew my hope,
   renew my faith in You;
   grant me strength that I may cope,
   and grace in all I do.

   Lift my spirit to the sky,
   Each day the sun's above;
   every night the moon is high,
   renew me with Your love.

   K. Kirkland

2. With untiring love you have watched over us
   from one year to the next.
   Unlike us, you don't grow weary or old,
   but remain steady and secure.
   For the light that never failed us
   and the grace that never left us
   in days gone by, we say thank you.
   At the dawn of each new day,
   shine upon us and may our hearts be kept strong
   by your hope. For Your name's sake. Amen.

   H. McIlveen

Note

You can use this theme as a New Year's program.

THANKSGIVING

Hymns

Anyone Who Eats This Bread
Alleluia, Give Thanks
The Butterfly Song
Can a Little Child Like Me?
Come, Ye Thankful People, Come
Count Your Blessings
Father, We Thank Thee
For All Your Goodness, God
For the Fruit of All Creation
For Thy Gracious Blessing
Harvest Hymn
Let All Things Now Living
Now Thank We All Our God
Rejoice, Ye Pure in Heart
Thank You
Thanks Be to God
Thanksgiving Blessing (words and music by Mary Lu Walker)
To Render Thanks Unto the Lord
We Gather Together to Ask the Lord's Blessing
We Thank Thee, Loving Father
When I Fall on My Knees

Secular Songs

Count Your Blessings (from the movie *White Christmas*)
Over the River and Through the Woods
Thanks for the Memory (Bob Hope's signature song)
This Glorious Food (also known as Vegetable Grace)
    (Patricia McKernon)
Wind Beneath My Wings (Bette Midler)

Story

The traditional story of the first white settlers in New England (or Canada), who in gratitude to God and the native people for their survival through a first year set aside a time for giving thanks and sharing the products of their labor.

Quotation

A thankful heart is not only the greatest virtue, but the parent of all other virtues.

Cicero

Discussion

1. If you counted your blessings, what would they be?
2. What's one thing that you are thankful for? (You may need to prompt them: children, family, friends, God, spouse, a personality trait, feeling loved.)
3. Are you thankful to be alive? Why or why not?
4. Discuss thankful expressions: thank heaven, thank God, thankless, no thanks to you, thank-you-ma'am (a bump or depression in the road), thanks for nothing, I will thank you to (leave me alone), he has only himself to thank, thanks offering.
5. Say grace: for what we are about to receive, O Lord, make us truly thankful.
6. What things do you find it difficult to give thanks for?

Sensory Cues

1. You might make a list of all the things the group is thankful for on a large easel. Individual thank-you cards that contain a specific reference to something you, as group leaders, are thankful for about that person are nice, especially with higher-functioning people who won't lose the card.
2. A cornucopia or horn of plenty can also be a symbol of Thanksgiving.

Prayer

Almighty God, Father of all mercies, we your servants give you thanks for all your goodness and loving-kindness to us and to all people. We bless you for our creation, preservation, and all the blessings of this life; but above all for your incomparable love in the redemption of the world by our Lord Jesus Christ, for the means of grace, and for the hope of glory. And, we pray, give us an awareness of your mercies, that with truly thankful hearts we may make known your praise, not only with our lips, but in our lives, by giving up ourselves to your service, and by walking before you in holiness and righteousness all our days; through Jesus Christ our Lord, to whom, with you and the Holy Spirit, be all honour and glory throughout the ages. Amen.

Traditional Anglican Prayer

VETERANS DAY/REMEMBRANCE DAY

Hymns

Abide with Me
Battle Hymn of the Republic
Lest We Forget
Let There Be Peace on Earth (close with this hymn)
O God, Our Help in Ages Past
Onward Christian Soldiers
Soldier, Soldier, Fighting in the World's Great Strife
The Son of God Goes Forth to War
St. Patrick's Breastplate
This Is a Time to Remember

You can also use hymns from "Death/Loss" for this session.

Secular Songs

Use a selection of World War I and II and related songs, such as:

Anchors Aweigh
The Caissons Go Rolling Along
Danny Boy
Don't Sit Under the Apple Tree
It's a Long Way to Tipperary
It's Been a Long, Long Time
Keep the Home Fires Burning
The Last Post (instrumental)
Over There
Pack Up Your Troubles (in Your Old Kit Bag)
Reveille (instrumental)
Roses of Picardy
(There'll Be Bluebirds Over) the White Cliffs of Dover
We'll Meet Again

Stories

1. Edith Cavell's last words, October 12, 1915, just before her execution by the Germans: "I realize that patriotism is not

enough. I must have no hatred or bitterness towards anyone."
Source: Bartlett, 1992, p. 590. See also Forgiveness, p. 38, for
further information about Cavell.

2. The story of how John McCrae came to write "In Flanders Fields"
   may be found on the World Wide Web at: *http://www.iaehv.nl/
   users/robr/poppies.html* and *http://hcs.harvard.edu/%7Ehgscc/
   html/flanders.html*

Poem

In Flanders Fields

In Flanders fields the poppies blow
Between the crosses, row on row,
That mark our place; and in the sky
The larks, still bravely singing, fly
Scarce heard amid the guns below.

We are the Dead. Short days ago
We lived, felt dawn, saw sunset glow,
Love and were loved, and now we lie,
In Flanders fields.

Take up our quarrel with the foe:
To you from failing hands we throw
The torch; be yours to hold it high.
If ye break faith with us who die
We shall not sleep, though poppies grow
In Flanders fields.

John McCrae, May 3, 1915

(Sources: *http://www.iaehv.nl/users/robr/poppies.html* and
http://hcs.harvard.edu/%7Ehgscc/html/flanders.html)

Quotations

1. Blessed are the peacemakers, for they will be called sons of
   God.

Matthew 5:9 (NIV)

2. You have heard that it was said, "Love your neighbor and hate your enemy." But I tell you: Love your enemies and pray for those who persecute you, that you may be sons of your Father in heaven.

Matthew 5:43-45 (NIV)

Discussion

1. Talk about memories of World War I and II. Did your father fight in the war? Brothers? Uncles? Did you help to build aircraft? (Remember that many women assisted in the war efforts too.)
2. What do you remember about World War I? World War II?
3. Did you serve in the war? (Remember that many women played an active part in the services.)
4. Do you remember hearing when World War II was declared? Where were you living then? How did you feel?
5. Some people of British, Continental European, and Oriental backgrounds will remember bombing raids or invading armies; questions about such experiences may evoke feelings of fear or adventure. For example, one woman living in England during World War II remembered the fear and drama of giving birth during an air raid with all the lights out!
6. You could ask about memories of rationing, food shortages, geographical dislocation, and knowledge of people killed in battle.

Sensory Cue

Provide a cross with poppies on it, military medals, pictures of uniformed personnel, an antique gun replica.

Prayer

Dear Lord, today we remember and honor all of those who have served our country so well. We remember the friends, the family, the unknown soldiers. We give thanks to those brave men and women who were willing to sacrifice everything for our freedom. Together we pray for peace everlasting, in Jesus' name. Amen.

K. Kirkland

Spiritual

ANGELS

Hymns

Angel Band
Angel Voices Ever Singing
Angels from the Realms of Glory
Angels Holy, Angels Lowly
Angels Hovering Round
Angels, Roll the Rock Away
Angels Watching Over Me
Angels We Have Heard On High
Christians Awake
The First Noel
Hark, Hark My Soul
Hark! The Herald Angels Sing
The Holy City
It Came Upon the Midnight Clear
May Flights of Angels Lead You
Songs of Praise the Angels Sang
Swing Low, Sweet Chariot
While Shepherds Watched Their Flocks by Night
Whispering Hope

Secular Songs

Down in the Valley (last 2 verses)
I Have a Dream (Abba)
My Special Angel
Wind Beneath My Wings (Bette Midler)

Stories

1. The angel Gabriel appearing to Zechariah (Luke 1:11-20) and later to Mary (Luke 1:26-38)

2. See Karen Goldman's *Angel Encounters* (Simon and Schuster, 1995)
3. An angel helping Peter to get out of prison—Acts 12:7-11,15
4. Contemporary stories of angels

Discussion

1. Do you believe in angels?
2. What do angels look like?
3. How does one become an angel?

Sensory Cue

Bring pictures of angels from Renaissance paintings to pass around the group. Use one picture at the start and see if they can name what it is a picture of.

Prayer

O everlasting God, who has ordained and constituted the services of Angels and people in a wonderful order; mercifully grant, that as Your holy Angels always do You service in heaven, so by Your appointment may they succor and defend us on earth; through Jesus Christ our Lord.

The Oxford Book of Prayer (p. 250)

CREATION/NATURE

Hymns

All Creatures of Our God and King
All Things Bright and Beautiful
Angels Holy, High and Lowly
Can a Little Child Like Me?
Fairest Lord Jesus
Father Eternal, Ruler of Creation
Father, Long Before Creation
For Beauty of Meadows
For the Beauty of the Earth
For the Fruit of All Creation
God Sees the Little Sparrow Fall (He Loves Me Too)
God Who Touches Earth with Beauty
The God Whom Earth and Sea and Sky
Heaven and Earth, and Sea and Air
How Great Thou Art (verse 2)
Morning Has Broken (especially verse 2)
Nature Glows with Colors Rare
O Father, All Creating
Sing to the Mountains
This Is My Father's World
We Thank You, God

Secular Songs

De Colores
Happy Wanderer
Mockingbird Hill
Oh, What a Beautiful Mornin' (from *Oklahoma!*)
This Land Is Your Land
What a Wonderful World (Louis Armstrong)

Stories

1. Jesus and a storm—Mark 4:35-41

2. You might supplement the story from Mark with contemporary experiences of the wonder, awe, or beauty in Creation—or of the experience of affecting nature through prayer.

Quotation

> Earth's crammed with heaven
> and every common bush afire with God;
> but only those who see take off their shoes,
> the rest sit around and pluck blackberries.

Elizabeth Barrett Browning
Sonnets from the Portuguese, Vol. 7, line 820

Discussion

1. Do you enjoy nature? Walking outdoors?
2. Did you ever have a cabin or go camping in the woods?
3. Mention local parks or scenic attractions that the group members might be familiar with; also, mention national attractions such as Niagara Falls, Yellowstone National Park, etc.
4. Do you love the sight of the ocean? The mountains? The wide-open plains? Fields of corn?
5. Sometimes nature strikes me as being so beautiful and wondrous that I feel closer to God and so grateful for Creation. Have you ever felt that way? Use the second verse from "How Great Thou Art," which refers to nature: "When thro' the woods and forest glades I wander . . . then sings my soul."

Sensory Cues

1. Bring branches with bright colorful leaves or fresh flowers. If the weather is good, hold the group meeting outside on a patio.
2. Discuss the wonder of creation as you pass around a flower—how it grows from seed, eventually blooming in beauty.

Prayer

Lord, isn't your creation wasteful? Fruits never equal the
  seedlings' abundance.
Springs scatter water. The sun gives out enormous light.
May your bounty teach me greatness of heart.
May your magnificence stop me being mean.
Seeing you a prodigal and open-handed giver,
Let me give unstintingly like a king's son, like God's own.

Helder Camara
The Hodder Book of Christian Prayers
(Castle, 1986, pp. 28-29)

THE CROSS

Hymns

At the Cross
Beneath the Cross of Jesus
Hallelujah! What A Savior!
The Holy City (verse 2 especially)
I Am Coming to the Cross
It Is Well with My Soul (verse 2)
Jesus, Keep Me Near the Cross
Lift High the Cross
Must Jesus Bear the Cross Alone?
The Old Rugged Cross
Onward, Christian Soldiers
"Take Up Your Cross," the Savior Said
There Is a Fountain Filled with Blood
There Is a Green Hill Far Away
The Way of the Cross Leads Home
Were You There When They Crucified My Lord?
When I Survey the Wondrous Cross

Story

Describe the process of Jesus being crucified—the crown of thorns; the beating, spitting, insulting; the pain and disgrace; the long process of dying—Matthew 27:27-50

Poem

Go to dark Gethsemane, Ye that feel the tempter's power;
Your Redeemer's conflict see; what with Him one bitter hour;
Turn not from His griefs away; learn of Jesus Christ to pray.

See Him at the judgment hall, beaten, bound, reviled, arraigned;
See Him meekly bearing all; love to man His soul sustained;
Shun not suffering, shame or loss; learn of Christ to bear the cross.

Calvary's mournful mountain climb; there adoring at His feet,
Mark that miracle of time, God's own sacrifice complete:
"It is finished!" hear Him cry; learn of Jesus Christ to die.

James Montgomery (1825)
(Hymn Book of the Anglican Church
of Canada, 1972, pp. 451-452)

Discussion

1. What does the cross mean to you?
2. What crosses have you had to bear in life?
3. Who is the person in your life who has sacrificed the most for you (mother, father, grandparent, spouse)? Why did that person do that for you? How did it help your life? Does the thought of all that person has done for you make you sad or glad?
4. Does the thought of what happened to Jesus make you sad or glad?

Sensory Cue

Bring a large cross to pass around at the start of group. Ask what it reminds them of, what it makes them think of. For some, the connection may be obvious to them and the cross's meaning apparent. For others, it will stir a deep memory.

Prayer

A verse or two from one of the hymns would be appropriate, e.g., "When I Survey the Wondrous Cross," or "Jesus, Keep Me Near the Cross":

> Near the cross I'll watch and wait, hoping, trusting ever,
> till I reach the golden strand just beyond the river.
> In the cross, in the cross, be my glory ever,
> till my raptured soul shall find Rest beyond the river. Amen.

HEALING

Hymns

Be Still and Know That I Am God (verse 2)
For the Healing of the Nations
God Will Take Care of You
The Great Physician
Guide Me, O Thou Great Jehovah (verse 2)
He Touched Me
The Healer
Healing at the Fountain
I Heard the Voice of Jesus Say
Jesus' Hands Were Kind Hands
Lay Your Hands
Living Where the Healing Waters Flow
The Lord That Healeth Thee
O Lord, By Thee Delivered
O Love That Will Not Let Me Go
Out of My Bondage, Sorrow and Night
Prayer of St. Francis (Make Me a Channel of Your Peace)
Someone Is Here with a Burden (verse 1)
There is a Balm in Gilead
Touch Him and Be Made Whole!
What a Friend We Have in Jesus

Secular Songs

Cry Like an Angel (Shawn Colvin)
I Will Stand Fast (Fred Small)
The Mary Ellen Carter (Stan Rodgers or Ian Robb)
A Row of Small Trees (Garnet Roger)
Sail On (Dick Gaughan)
Turning Toward the Morning (Gordon Bok)
When My Boat Is Built Again (Cormac McCarthy)

Stories

1. Jesus heals the paralytic—Mark 2:1-12
2. Various hymn stories (see Osbeck, 1982)

Discussion

1. Do you carry a hurt or sorrow you would like to heal?
2. Have you ever had surgery?
3. If you could heal something in yourself, what would it be?
4. Have you ever prayed for someone to be healed when they were sick? What happened?
5. Do you believe in miracles? Have you ever experienced a miracle?
6. Talk about healing waters and places such as Lourdes.

Sensory Cue

Bring an herbal remedy or healing ointment with a distinct smell, such as camphor, for the people to smell, possibly stimulating memories. Discuss how it is used for healing purposes.

Prayer

If you (and the resident) feel comfortable with hands-on prayer, especially with someone who is particularly in need of healing, you might do so as part of this theme.
You could use the hymn "Lay Your Hands" during this time.

> Jesus, when you were here on Earth you reached out, touched people, and made them whole. Reach out now through us and make us well—emotionally, spiritually, and physically, for your name's sake. Amen.

H. McIlveen

Note

You might also begin the group by relating a story of someone you know or read about who had a healing experience, during which it seemed that a miracle took place.

HEAVEN

Hymns

Amazing Grace
Beyond the Sunset
Deep River
Heaven Is My Home
In the Sweet By-and-By
Jesus Loves Me
Precious Lord, Take My Hand
Shall We Gather at the River?
Softly and Tenderly Jesus Is Calling
Soon and Very Soon
Swing Low, Sweet Chariot
When the Roll Is Called Up Yonder
When the Saints Go Marching In
When We All Get to Heaven

Secular Songs

Beautiful Isle of Somewhere
Get Happy
Tears in Heaven (Eric Clapton)

Stories

1. Read and discuss Jesus' words in John 14:1-4.
2. Talk about near-death or after-death experiences that others have reported or the experiences of yourself or someone you know who has "seen" heaven.

Discussion

1. Jesus said, "I go to prepare a place for you." What kind of place would you like him to prepare for you? What sounds would you like to hear there (talk about music, birdsong, running water)? What sights (flowers, scenery)? What animals (pets)? What

people (spouse, parents)? What smells and scents (flowers, oven-baked bread)?

2. Spark the imagination of the group: Would Jesus be there? What would it be like to meet Him? To touch Him? Can you imagine the hands of Jesus upon you? How would you feel?

Sensory Cue

Show pictures that might be suggestive of an image of heaven: a picture of a glorious sunrise through colorful clouds and sky; a large wrought-iron gate; a mansion; an Eden-like garden with joyous people.

Prayer

If possible, have one of the group members assist or lead the recitation of The Lord's Prayer.

LIFE AFTER DEATH

Hymns

Because He Died and Is Risen
Because He Lives
The Day of Resurrection
Hail the Day That Sees Him Rise
Hallelujah! Jesus Lives
He Lives
I Know That My Redeemer Lives
In the Resurrection
Jesus Christ Is Risen Today
Jesus Comes with All His Grace
Like the Golden Sun
Morning Has Broken
Thine Is the Glory, Risen, Conquering Son

Secular Songs

Don't Cry (Guns 'n' Roses)
Forever Young (Joan Baez)
I Have a Dream
I'll Be There (Escape Club)
Lamplight Symphony (Kansas)
Life (Tom Paxton)
Tears in Heaven (Eric Clapton)

Stories

1. The story of the vision of Nathan, a seven-year-old boy who died of a liver problem (McIlveen, 1992, pp. 6-7)
2. The account of a dying sixteen-year-old girl who revives, says words such as "I see him; I'm going to him," then falls back on the pillow and dies (Osis and Haraldsson, 1977, pp. 34-35)

Quotations

1. All I want is to know Christ and to experience the power of his resurrection, to share in his sufferings and become like him in his death, in the hope that I myself will be raised from death to life.

Philippians 3:10-11

2. He is not here: for He is risen, as He said. Come, see the place where the Lord lay.

Luke 24:5-6

Discussion

1. In the Bible, in the book of Job (14:14), Job asks, "If a man dies, will he live again?" What do you think? Do you believe in life after death? What do you imagine it's like? How would it feel? Where do we go after we die? How do you feel about dying? In some cultures a death is celebrated—why do you think they would celebrate?
2. What would you like people to remember you for? What is one thing you'd like to be remembered for?
3. Job later answered his own question (an answer that is also a hymn): "I know that my Redeemer lives, and that in the end He will stand upon the earth. And after my skin has been destroyed, yet in my flesh I will see God; I myself will see Him with my own eyes."—Job 19:25-27.

Sensory Cue

Plant a bulb or seed together as a group, perhaps a lily, as a symbol of new life.

Prayer

Almighty God: Grant that, as your only-begotten Son, our Lord Jesus Christ, ascended into the heavens, so may we also ascend there in heart and mind, to dwell continually with him, who lives and reigns with you and the Holy Spirit, one God, world without end. Amen.

(adapted from *Service Book,* p. 126)

Note

You might discuss how different cultures view death and what they believe happens afterward. If your group has a mix of faiths or backgrounds, discuss their individual opinions openly and with acceptance.

PEACE

Hymns

Dear Lord and Father of Mankind
Dona Nobis Pacem
Father of Peace
Go Now in Peace
He Whispers Sweet Peace to Me
Hidden Peace
It Is Well with My Soul
Let There Be Peace on Earth
Now Let Us Depart in Peace
Peace
Peace, Be Still
Peace I Leave
Peace Is Flowing Like a River
Peace, Perfect Peace
Peace Prayer
Prayer of St. Francis (Make Me a Channel of Your Peace)
Shalom, My Friends, Shalom
There'll Be Peace in the Valley

Use also hymns of a peaceful nature or those which are peaceful to certain individuals in the group.

Secular Songs

From a Distance (Bette Midler)
Give Peace a Chance
Happy Christmas/War Is Over (John Lennon)
Ninety-Nine Red Balloons
One Tin Soldier
Oseh Shalom
Peace of the River (words by Janet E. Tobitt)
Shalom Chaverim
(There'll Be Bluebirds Over) the White Cliffs of Dover
Vine and Fig Tree (Lo Yisa Goy)

Story

Jesus and a storm—Mark 4:35-41

Discussion

1. What kinds of things make you feel peaceful? Cue them with suggestions: tactile objects (an afghan, a teddy bear, a cat, a warm hand), sound (birds in the trees, the surf, gentle music), places (a sandy beach, church, a warm bed, your own home, an ocean view), reassurance (friends, compliments, affirmations of faith, kind words).
2. Would you describe your life as having been peaceful? Is it peaceful now? Why or why not?
3. Discuss times of war and peace.
4. Reminisce about places that feel or felt peaceful: going to church, a garden, a park, a vacation.
5. What would bring you a sense of peace today (love, support, someone to sit with, a stroll)?
6. Discuss the quotation, "A heart at peace gives life to the body."—Proverbs 14:30

Sensory Cue

Pass around comforting items such as a knitted blanket or a teddy bear and symbols of peace such as a picture of a dove.

Poem

Read "Peace, Be Still" by M. Elizabeth Coulson (MacHugh, 1938).

> I found a spot of beauty rare,
> Both God and nature lingered there,
> And in the quiet of the hill
> I heard God whisper, "Peace, be still."
> In the deep arch of blue above
> I read of His unbounded love,

While in the murmur of the trees
The gentle rustling of the trees
I heard His voice speak low and sweet:
"Fear not, my child, go forth and meet
Life squarely, for it is My will,
Receive My blessing: 'Peace, be still.'"

Prayers

1. The Lord bless you and keep you. The Lord make his face shine upon you and be gracious to you. The Lord lift up his countenance upon you, and give you peace. Amen.

Numbers 6:26 (NKJV)

2. Lead me from unreal to real,
   from darkness to light,
   from death to immortality.
   Peace, Peace, Peace.

Om Shanti Mantra

Note

The turmoil and "craziness" of a dementia unit can often lack an experience of peace. Use this theme as an opportunity to create this feeling. It's useful both on days that match this mood or when the unit is tense and hectic.

PRAYER

Hymns

All the Way My Savior Leads Me
Father, Hear the Prayer We Offer
God Is So Good
He Prayed
I Am Praying for You
It's Me, It's Me, Oh Lord
Kum By Yah
The Lord's Prayer
Pause for a Moment of Prayer
Peace Prayer
Prayer Is the Soul's Sincere Desire
Prayer of St. Francis (Make Me a Channel of Your Peace)
Shalom, My Friends, Shalom
Spirit Divine, Attend Our Prayers
Standing in the Need of Prayer (It's Me)
Sweet Hour of Prayer
Teach Me to Pray, Lord
What a Friend We Have in Jesus
Whisper a Prayer

Secular Songs

I Say a Little Prayer (Dionne Warwick)
Just a Baby's Prayer at Twilight
My Prayer
On a Wing and a Prayer

Stories

1. Luke 11:1-10. (Demonstrate knocking on the door of the room as it relates to the biblical passage. You can also sing "The Lord's Prayer" (the Molotte rendition).
2. Christ before the Crucifixion—Luke 22:39-53

Discussion

1. Remind them of this childhood poem: "Now I lay me down to sleep, I pray the Lord my soul to keep. If I should die before I wake, I pray the Lord my soul to take."
2. Do you pray? Does it help? What happens when you pray? Do you pray for others?
3. Who do you talk to when you pray?
4. Mark 11:23-24 quotes Jesus saying, "Whatsoever you desire, when you pray, believe that you receive them, and you shall have them." Have you ever had this experience? What if we tried that right now (perhaps for one person in particular)?

Sensory Cues

1. Bring a picture of Christ praying in the Garden of Gethsemane or a picture of a person or family praying.
2. Tell the story behind the hymn "All the Way My Savior Leads Me," written by Fanny Crosby in thanks to God for answering a prayer (Osbeck, 1982, p. 25).

Prayer

What was the first prayer you ever learned? Was it "Now I lay me down to sleep . . . "? Talk/ask about what we do with our hands, eyes, and heads when we pray; demonstrate praying—kneeling, head bowed, hands together. Explore memorized prayers: "Now I lay me down to sleep, I pray Thee, Lord, thy child to keep; Thy love guard me through the night and wake me with the morning light" or The Lord's Prayer. Do you pray? Did you pray? This may be a good opportunity to pray for particular individuals and for the laying on of hands.

Note

There may be a group member who is willing and able to lead the group in prayer. Encourage someone to do this when possible.

APPENDIXES

Blank Theme Pages

HYMNS

SECULAR SONGS

STORIES

QUOTATIONS

DISCUSSION

SENSORY CUES

POEMS

PRAYERS

NOTES

Hymnal Sources

Beckwith, Paul (Ed.) (1952). *Hymns.* Chicago, IL: Inter-Varsity Press.

Bristol Jr., Lee Hastings, and Friedell, Harold William (Eds.) (1953). *Hymns for Children and Grownups to Use Together.* New York: Farrar, Straus, and Young.

Catholic Book of Worship II, Choir Edition (1980). Ottawa: Concacan Inc.

Choice Hymns of the Faith (1969). Kansas City, KS: Gospel Perpetuating Publishers.

Ehret, Walter, Edwards, Melinda, and Evans, George K. (Eds.) (1969). *The International Book of Sacred Song.* Englewood Cliffs, NJ: Prentice-Hall, Inc., pp. 197-198.

Giesbrecht, Carol M. (Ed.) (1973). *The Hymnal.* Canada: The Baptist Federation of Canada, p. 86.

The Hymn Book of the Anglican Church of Canada and the United Church of Canada (1972). Toronto, ON: Southam Printing Ltd.

Hymns Ancient and Modern Revised (1972). London: William Clowes and Sons, Ltd.

Hymns of Glorious Praise (1969). Springfield, MO: Gospel Publishing House.

Hymns of Universal Praise (1981). Kowloon, Hong Kong: Chinese Christian Literature Council, Ltd.

Life Song: A Hymnal for Church, School, and Family (1982). Trumansburg, NY: K & R Music, Inc.

The Lutheran Hymnal (1941). St. Louis, MO: Concordia Publishing House.

Melodies of Praise (1957). Springfield, MO: Gospel Publishing House.

The Methodist Hymnal (1939). Baltimore, MD: The Methodist Publishing House.

National Council for Liturgy (Ed.) (1972). *Catholic Book of Worship.* Toronto, ON: Gordon V. Thompson, Ltd.

Psalter Hymnal: Centennial Edition (1959). Grand Rapids, MI: Publication Committee of the Christian Reformed Church, Inc.

Revivalaires: McColl-Gerard Revival Songs (1949). Jacksonville, FL: Stamps-Baxter Music and Printing Company.

The Singing Church (1987). Carol Stream, IL: Hope Publishing Company.

Smith, Alfred B. (Ed.) (1944). *Action Songs for Boys and Girls.* Grand Rapids, MI: Zondervan Publishing House.

Songs for a Gospel People (1987). Winfield, BC: Wood Lake Books, Inc.

Stringfield, R.W., Moore, Ray H., Stevens, Roy F., Ramquist, A.E., Williams, R.T., and Hawkins, Floyd W. (1958). *Rejoice and Sing!* Kansas City, MO: Lillenas Publishing Company.

Whitmore, Alan C. (Ed.) (1995). *Hymns We Love to Sing.* Louiseville, Quebec: Wood Lake Books.

Worship and Service Hymnal (1966). Chicago, IL: Hope Publishing Company.

Woychuk, N.A. (Ed.) (1969). *Making Melody.* St. Louis, MO: Bible Memory Association International.

Bibliography

Ahsen, Akhter (1992). "Imagery of prayer: A pilot experiment on concepts and content," *Journal of Mental Imagery*, 16(3/4), 1-72.

Appleton, George (1985). *The Oxford Book of Prayer*. New York: Oxford University Press.

Atkinson, Steve (1998). "Churchgoers live longer, are happier," *Nanaimo Daily News*, July 4, D7.

Bartlett, John (1992). In Justin Kaplan (Ed.), *Familiar Quotations*. Boston: Little, Brown and Company, pp. 438, 590.

Bell, Lettice and Le Feuvre, Amy (1941). *Our Risen Lord*. London: A.B. Shaw and Company.

Blazer, Dan (1991). "Spirituality and aging well," *Generations*. Winter, 61-65.

Book of Common Prayer (1962). Aylesbury, England: BPCC Hazell Books.

Canadian Association for Music Therapy (1992). "Music therapy: A health care profession," brochure.

Carr, Katherine K. (1993). "Integration of spirituality of aging into a nursing curriculum," *Gerontology and Geriatrics Education*, 13(3), 33-46.

Carson, George S. (1907). *Stories from the Life of Jesus*. Toronto, ON: R. Douglas Fraser.

Castle, Tony (1986). *The Hodder Book of Christian Prayers*. London: Hodder and Stoughton.

Clark, Peter Yuichi (1993). "A liturgical journey at Wesly Woods: Worship experiences within an inpatient geriatric psychiatric unit," *The Journal of Pastoral Care*, 47(4), 388-403.

Comfort, Alex (1976). *A Good Age*. London, England: Mitchell Beazley Publishers, Ltd.

Conn, Heather. "Early coastal explorers." In Davis, Chuck (Ed.), *The Greater Vancouver Book*. Vancouver, BC: The Linkman Press. Online. July 1, 1998. Available: *http://www.discovervancouver.com/vancouverbook/earlyex3.html*

Cooper, B. Lee and Haney, Wayne S. (1995). *Rock Music in American Popular Culture*. Binghamton, NY: Harrington Park Press.

Cooper, B. Lee and Haney, Wayne S. (1997). *Rock Music in American Popular Culture II*. Binghamton, NY: Harrington Park Press.

Coulson, M. Elizabeth (1938). "Peace, be still." In MacHugh, Edward (Ed.), *Edward MacHugh's Treasury of Gospel Hymns and Poems*. Winona Lake, IN: The Rodeheaver Hall-Mack Company.

Everett, Deborah (1996). *Forget Me Not*. Edmonton, Alberta: Inkwell Press.

Flora, Harpal. "Diwali." Online. June 29, 1998. Available: *http://www.greenchilli.mcmail.com/DIWALI.html*

Gabriel, Charles H. (1952). "My evening prayer." In George, David L. (Ed.), *The Family Book of Best-Loved Poems.* Garden City, NY: Hanover House, pp. 58-59.

George, David L. (Ed.) (1952). *The Family Book of Best-Loved Poems.* Garden City, NY: Hanover House.

Gerdner, Linda A. and Swanson, Elizabeth A. (1993). "Effects of individualized music on confused and agitated elderly patients," *Archives of Psychiatric Nursing,* VII(5), October, 284-291.

God's Promises for Your Every Need (no date). Houston, TX: Living Scriptures, Inc.

Goldman, Karen (1995). *Angel Encounters: Real Stories of Angelic Intervention.* New York: Simon and Schuster.

Hamilton, Edith (1942). *Mythology.* Boston: Little, Brown and Company, pp. 27, 296-297.

Hamlyn, Harvey (Ed.) (1932). *The Joys of Fellowship.* New York: George Sully and Company, pp. 11, 15.

Hansel, Tim (1985). *You Gotta Keep Dancing.* Elgin, IL: David C. Cook Publishing Company.

Hansel, Tim (1991). *Through the Wilderness of Loneliness.* Elgin, IL: David C. Cook Publishing Company.

Heriot, Cathy S. (1992). "Spirituality and aging," *Holistic Nursing Practice,* 7(1), 22-31.

"The history of Hannukah" (sic). Online. June 29, 1998. Available: *http://www.ort.org/ort/hanukkah/history.html*

Jones, W. Paul (1984). "Aging as a spiritualizing process," *Journal of Religion and Aging,* 1(1), 3-16.

Kerr, Hugh and Mulder, John (Eds.) (1983). *Conversions.* Grand Rapids, MI: Eerdmans, pp. 4-10.

Koenig, Harold G. (1990). "Research on religion and mental health in later life: A review and commentary," *Journal of Geriatric Psychiatry,* 23(1), 23-53.

Komp, Diane (1992). *A Window to Heaven.* Grand Rapids, MI: Zondervan Publishing House.

Lynch, Charles (1983). *You Can't Print That.* Edmonton, Alberta: Hurtig Press.

MacHugh, Edward (Ed.) (1938). *Edward MacHugh's Treasury of Gospel Hymns and Poems.* Winona Lake, IN: The Rodeheaver Hall-Mack Company.

Martin, Diane S. and Fuller, Wendy G. (1991). "Spirituality and aging: Activity key to 'holiest' health care," *Activities, Adaptation, and Aging,* 15(4), 37-50.

Martin, Robert (1989). *My Journey into Alzheimer's.* Wheaton, IL: Tyndale House.

McFadden, Susan H. and Gerl, Robert R. (1990). "Approaches to understanding spirituality in the second half of life," *Generations,* Fall, 35-38.

McIlveen, Esther (1992). "Look home angel," *Vancouver Sun,* November 21, C6-C7.

Merriam-Webster's Biographical Dictionary (1995). Springfield, MA: Merriam-Webster, Inc., p. 192.

Nikles, Robin (1994). "Integration of music therapy and theology: A preliminary approach," *The Australian Journal of Music Therapy, 52-56.*

Osbeck, Kenneth W. (Ed.) (1982). *101 Hymn Stories.* Grand Rapids, MI: Kregel Publications.

Osbeck, Kenneth W. (Ed.) (1985). *101 More Hymn Stories.* Grand Rapids, MI: Kregel Publications.

Osis, Karlis and Haraldsson, Erlendur (1977). *At the Hour of Death.* New York: Avon, pp. 34-35.

"Our Daily Bread: Working in God's garden," July 1, 1998. Online. July 12, 1998. Grand Rapids, MI: RBC Ministries. Available: *http://www.gospelcom.net/rbc/ odb/odb-07-01-98.html*

"Our Daily Bread: Working in God's garden," July 6, 1998. Online. July 12, 1998. Grand Rapids, MI: RBC Ministries. Available: *http://www.gospelcom.net/rbc/ odb/odb-07-06-98.html*

Pargament, Kenneth I., Olsen, Hannah, Reilly, Barbara, Falgout, Kathryn, Ensing, David S., and Van Haitsma, Kimberly (1992). "God help me (II): The relationship of religious orientations to religious coping with negative life events," *Journal for the Scientific Study of Religion,* 31(4), 504-513.

Pratt, Michael W., Hunsberger, Bruce, Pancer, S. Mark, and Roth, Dan (1992). "Reflections on religion: Aging, belief, orthodoxy, and interpersonal conflict in the complexity of adult thinking about religious issues," *Journal for the Scientific Study of Religion,* 31(4), 514-522.

Rodeheaver, Homer A., Sanville, George W., Rodeheaver, Yumbert P., and Rodeheaver, Joseph N. (Eds.) (1934). *Triumphant Service Songs,* Chicago, IL: The Rodeheaver Hall-Mack Company, pp. 262, 265, 268.

Roller, Bill and Nelson, Vivian (1991). *The Art of Co-Therapy.* New York: The Guilford Press.

Service Book for the Use of Ministers Conducting Public Worship (1983). Canada: Canec Publishing and Supply House.

Stem-Owens, Virginia (1993). "The dark side of grace," *Christianity Today,* July 19, pp. 32-35.

Studwell, William (1994). *The Popular Song Reader.* Binghamton, NY: The Haworth Press, Inc.

Studwell, William (1995). *The Christmas Carol Reader,* Binghamton, NY: The Haworth Press, Inc.

Studwell, William (1996). *The National and Religious Song Reader.* Binghamton, NY: The Haworth Press, Inc.

Studwell, William (1997). *The Americana Song Reader.* Binghamton, NY: The Haworth Press, Inc.

Tillett, Beverly (Ed.) (1975). *Jerry Silverman's Folk Song Encyclopedia, Volume Two.* New York: Chapell Music Company.

Williams, Margery (1985). *The Velveteen Rabbit.* New York: Smithmark Pubs., Inc.

Young, Cathy (1993). "Spirituality and the chronically ill Christian elderly," *Geriatric Nursing,* November/December, 298-303.

General Index

Index of
Hymns and Secular Songs